The Life and Times of the Steamboat *Red Cloud* or How Merchants, Mounties, and the Missouri Transformed the West

ED RACHAL FOUNDATION NAUTICAL ARCHAEOLOGY SERIES

In Association with the Institute of Nautical Archaeology

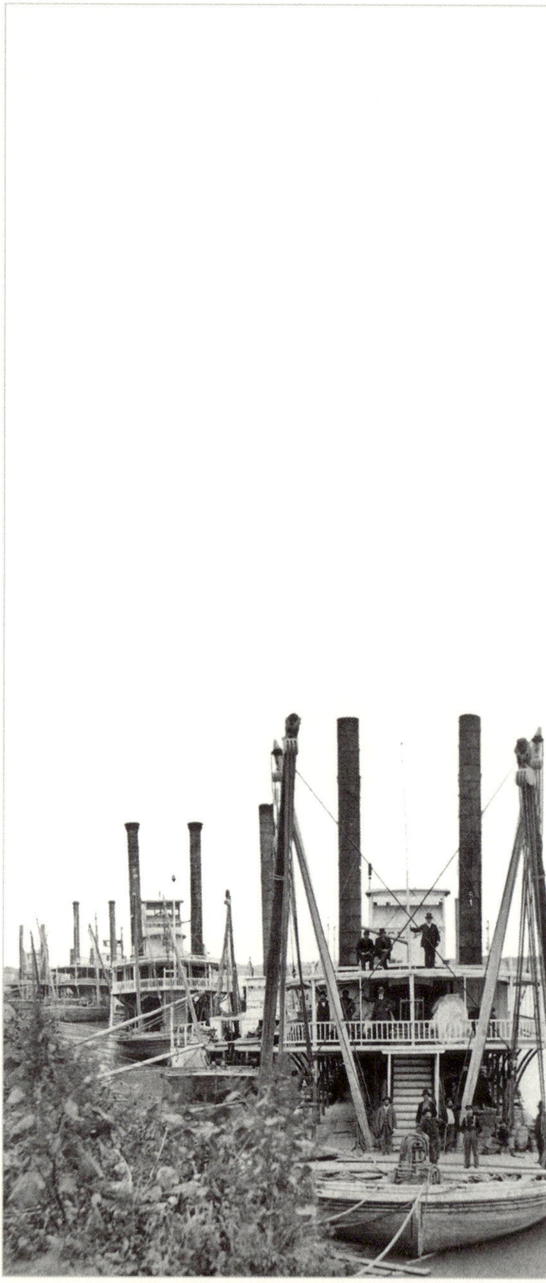

THE LIFE AND TIMES OF THE STEAMBOAT RED CLOUD

or

How Merchants, Mounties, *and the* Missouri *Transformed the West*

Annalies Corbin

Foreword by William E. Lass

TEXAS A&M UNIVERSITY PRESS
College Station

First edition

The paper used in this book meets the minimum requirements
of the American National Standard for Permanence
of Paper for Printed Library Materials, Z39.48-1984.
Binding materials have been chosen for durability.
∞

Library of Congress Cataloging-in-Publication Data

Corbin, Annalies.
The life and times of the steamboat Red Cloud, or, How merchants, mounties, and the Missouri transformed the West / Annalies Corbin ; foreword by William E. Lass.—1st ed.
p. cm. — (Ed Rachal Foundation nautical archaeology series)
Includes bibliographical references and index.
ISBN 1-58544-484-7 (cloth : alk. paper) — ISBN 1-58544-516-9 (pbk. : alk. paper)
1. Inland water transportation—Missouri River—History—19th century. 2. River steamers—Missouri River—History—19th century. 3. Red Cloud (Steamboat)—History. 4. Business enterprises—Montana—Fort Benton—History—19th century. 5. I. G. Baker and Company—History. 6. Frontier and pioneer life—Missouri River Region. 7. North West Mounted Police (Canada)—History—19th century. 8. Prairie Provinces—History—19th century. I. Title: Life and times of the steamboat Red Cloud. II. Title: How merchants, mounties, and the Missouri transformed the West. III. Title. IV. Series.
HE630.M63C67 2006
386'.22436—dc22
2005020767

For my devoted husband
Chip,
and dedicated to the memory of
Joel F. Overholser and
Michael P. Malone.

Contents

Illustrations

MAPS

TABLES

Foreword

During their westward expansion, Americans followed waterways whenever possible. Beyond the Mississippi, the Missouri River was the greatest natural highway into the vast West. All or parts of it were used by explorers; fur traders; Argonauts bound for California, Colorado, and Montana; and settlers on their way to Oregon.

Nineteenth-century American occupation of the Trans-Mississippi West was facilitated by the transportation revolution. In 1807, a year after explorers Meriwether Lewis and William Clark completed their twenty-eight-month round trip from St. Louis to the Pacific by way of the Missouri and Columbia rivers, Robert Fulton demonstrated a practical steamboat on the Hudson River.

Westerners, anxious to expand and speed commerce between Pittsburgh and New Orleans, welcomed the new technology. Fulton and his New York associates sent the *New Orleans,* the West's first steamboat, from Pittsburgh to New Orleans in 1811. Six years later, steam navigation was extended to St. Louis in 1817 with the arrival of the *Zebulon M. Pike.*

Successful steamboating on the Ohio and lower Mississippi emboldened Secretary of War John C. Calhoun to use steamers for military and scientific expeditions up the Missouri in 1819. Like most forward-thinking Americans, Calhoun saw the boats as the ultimate manifestation of American enterprise, ingenuity, and civilization. They would, he reasoned, impress upon the Indians and trespassing British traders that the United States had the technological means to bind the remote West to the rest of the nation.

Calhoun, like everyone else who relied on steamboats, soon found that while they were an improvement over previous craft, they had shortcomings. Potentially, they offered unprecedented speed and carrying capacity, but they were also prone to mechanical failures, groundings, snaggings and explosions. But, despite its limitations, steamboating, until the advent of railroads, provided the best available transportation. The poor performances of steamers on the 1819 government expeditions contributed to a renewed determination by builders and navigators to adapt their boats to shallow, hazardous western streams.

Over the course of four decades, steamboating was extended up the Missouri to Fort Benton, Montana, the practical head of navigation about thirty miles below the Great Falls. The American Fur Company was the principal catalyst for pushing steamboating far upstream. In 1831, the *Yellow Stone,* its first steamer, reached Fort Tecumseh near present-day Fort Pierre, South Dakota. The next year the boat made a round trip to Fort Union near the mouth of the Yellowstone River. Fort Union, an estimated 1,800 miles by the circuitous river from St. Louis, remained the main goal of traders for about twenty years. Then in the 1850s, Pierre Chouteau Jr. and Company, the successor of the American Fur Company, vigorously strove to get steamboats to Fort Benton. Aside from serving its own trade, the Chouteau Company was motivated by the federal government's desire to use the Missouri River as the longest segment of a northern route to the Pacific Northwest. Seeing the steamboat as an instrument of expansion, federal officials encouraged Chouteau and other civilian contractors.

In 1859 the Chouteau Company's *Chippewa* was navigated to within twelve miles of Fort Benton. The event, heralded as the completion of a long quest by American civilization to conquer the wilderness, was regarded as proof that modern machines were vital to fulfilling the nation's expansionist destiny.

While the *Chippewa* and its immediate successors were reigning on the upper river, Missouri River commerce was being affected by railroads. National agitation for a transcontinental railroad, which was spurred by the California gold rush, caused a flurry of railroad planning in Missouri. Missourians, with their history of being the gateway to the West, assumed railroads would solidify the hold of St. Louis over a great hinterland stretching toward the Pacific.

The trade pattern on the lower river was first altered by the opening of the Missouri Pacific Railroad from St. Louis to Jefferson City in 1857 and the completion of the Hannibal and St. Joseph Railroad two years later. Despite these advances, St. Louis remained the mistress of Missouri River steamboating. As such the city benefited immensely from the prosperous, long-haul "mountain trade" to Fort Benton during the Montana gold rush of the late 1860s.

But the advent of railroads on the upper Missouri created new ports within Chicago's trade area. In short order, Chicago-based railroads reached Sioux City, Iowa, in 1868 and Yankton and Bismarck in Dakota Territory five years later. The effect of these extensions was to make railroad-steamboat combinations the dominant trade pattern for the upper Missouri region. Fortunately for steamboatmen, the Panic of 1873 and ensuing dull times slowed railroad construction, which added to the importance of Bismarck and Yankton.

One of the most dramatic events in the entire history of Missouri River steamboating was the revival of the Fort Benton trade after the Northern Pacific Railroad reached Bismarck. With the end of the Montana gold rush and the completion of the transcontinental Union Pacific Railroad, it seemed that Fort Benton's glory days were over. But it boomed again because of events in the Canadian West.

The occupation of Canada's West was delayed by the monopolistic hold of the Hudson's Bay Company, which tended to suppress other enterprises. Thoughts of making Canada a transcontinental nation were aroused by the Fraser River gold rush in British Columbia in the late 1850s. But even after that event American expansionists, based mainly in St. Paul, Minnesota, aspired to annex Canada. Canada's future was assured when it was granted dominion status by Great Britain in 1867. This unprecedented degree of independence occurred as nationalistic Canadians were becoming much more interested in forging an ocean-to-ocean nation. To assure Canada's economic and political stability, its leaders negotiated the purchase of Rupert's Land, the holdings of the Hudson's Bay Company.

The acquisition of the West brought Canada a host of new problems. It suddenly inherited an immense, isolated domain peopled in part by refugee Indians from the United States, who still depended on American traders who poured across the unguarded international boundary.

This law-and-order crisis prompted the formation of the Royal Canadian Mounted Police in 1873. The first contingent of Mounties was sent overland to the area north of Montana, but Canadian officials soon realized they could best be supplied and reinforced by way of Fort Benton. Thus, Missouri River steamboating became a significant factor in the conquest of the West north of the border as well as that south of the border.

Annalies Corbin's fine work concentrates on the *Red Cloud,* the principal steamboat of I. G. Baker & Company of Fort Benton. In detailing the history of the vessel, she excellently describes how steamboat technology was vital in transforming a large portion of the Canadian West. Her lucidly written account contributes to an enhanced understanding of frontier transportation as well as American-Canadian commerce and relations.

William E. Lass
Professor Emeritus of History
Minnesota State University, Mankato

Preface

Although volumes have been written about the history of the American West, there remains much to uncover concerning the hidden maritime history of America's inland rivers, especially the history that sank with the hundreds of steamboat wrecks and related sites on the upper Missouri River between 1819 and 1920. These physical archives, in the form of shipwrecks, contain a forgotten archaeological legacy—a legacy that can add a great deal to our understanding of the old West.

In this book I examine the record of the steamboat *Red Cloud,* which operated on the Missouri River from 1877 until it sank in 1882. The *Red Cloud* is, in many ways, a reflection of the West through which it traveled. Its owner, I. G. Baker & Company, was one of the West's most influential mercantile firms. The life and times of the company's flagship tells volumes about the communities it serviced and the people it conveyed in an ever-changing and expanding western landscape.

American *manifest destiny,* as played out on the landscape of the West, showed great promise for the country as a whole. Taming the land and its resources became an obsession facilitated by the encroachment of transportation systems into new western territory. The competition for the easiest, fastest, and cheapest route from east to west was an evolutionary process spanning half a century from the early fur trade in the 1820s through the days of hard-rock mining in the 1860s. The discovery of gold in the Rocky Mountains intensified the push into the area and spawned great activity along the Missouri River. With an interest in exploiting the West's resources, transportation networks were created to handle the flow of goods and people in and out of newly formed communities.

Previous research concerning western transportation focused on the history of America's well-known trails, such as the Santa Fe and the Oregon, as the main "highways" through which people and goods moved west. The Oregon Trail, for example, was heavily utilized as a highway of western movement and was, consequently, heavily researched and documented. The Oregon Trail was not, however, the most heavily utilized or the most efficient pathway for the movement of people and goods into the unsettled region. The Missouri River system, as a corridor of expansion, is a landscape that demands attention and research as an immigration highway to the American far West.

Once the race to the West was on, several enterprising companies quickly saw the value of utilizing the Missouri River as its primary mode for moving goods and people through the region. Companies emerged and declined as they competed for raw materials, lucrative markets, and men with enough vision to risk it all on a turbulent river. Men like Isaac G. Baker, Thomas Power, William Kountz, and a handful of others were those with lasting impact. Like many western enterprises, I. G. Baker & Company saw its fortunes rise and fall with the ever-shifting currents of the extraction industries and communities the company serviced. Both proved to be nimble enterprises. Through clever positioning and resourcefulness, however, I. G. Baker & Company managed to create trends rather than simply responding to them. The company's steamboat, the *Red Cloud,* was instrumental in its business strategy in the region. Bringing people and supplies into the upper Missouri region, and taking gold and goods back down river to established markets, the *Red Cloud* both witnessed history and influenced some of its own.

The *Red Cloud* and I. G. Baker & Company are used as case studies in understanding and appreciating the development of the upper Missouri West. Through their activities we see trade, transportation, and population patterns that shaped both the past and present. This story begins and ends in the same place, with a shipwreck. The focus of this book is on identifying and understanding an often-forgotten past, and reevaluating the significance of a new future. The further study of the many sunken steamboats and their artifacts can bring a new understanding of the life and times of the western settlers in the region. The stories of many are buried under and around the ever-shifting Missouri River.

My research was possible with assistance from many people. Local historian and researcher Joel Overholser of Fort Benton, Montana, deserves a special thanks for sharing his passion for the history of the Missouri River with me, as well as his archival files at the Montana Agricultural Museum. His death is a sad personal event for me and a profound professional loss for all interested in the history of the region. The staff at the Montana Historical Society was especially helpful as were the staffs at the St. Louis Mercantile Library and the Missouri Historical Society in St. Louis; the North Dakota Historical Society at Bismarck; the Murphy Library in La Crosse, Wisconsin; the National Archives in Washington, D.C., and the Canadian National Archives in Ottawa. Without the constant attention and interest in this project from the personnel at those facilities, this research would not have been possible.

I would also like to thank Jack Custer of Steamboat Masters and Associates, and Jack Lepley of the Montana Agricultural Museum, as well as Larry Murphy, Dan Lenihan, and Matthew Russell of the Submerged Cultural Resources Unit, National Park Service, who were always supportive of my research efforts. Jack Scott and Nathan Richards are responsible for the beautiful maps found in this text. Special thanks goes to William Lass, Kent Hackmann, Cynthia Schwenk, Doug Scott, Brad Rodgers, Steve Dasovich, Mike Cussler, Andy Hall, and Sheli Smith for their suggestions and unfailing support. I thank my research assistants, Chris Valvano and Calvin Meyers, for the many trips to the library to track down sources and odd bits of missing information.

I express my deepest appreciation to Carlos Schwantes and Roderick Sprague for having faith in this work. Without both of them, it would not have been possible to continue my interest in the Missouri River West. Thanks also goes to Katherine Aiken, of the University of Idaho, and to Michael Malone, of Montana State University, for the time and effort they contributed to making suggestions for improving this work. I am honored by President Malone's interest in my work and his willingness to serve on my doctoral committee. He is sorely missed.

Financial support for this project came from Sons and Daughters of Pioneer Rivermen, who administer the J. Mack Gamble Fund, the Charles Redd Center for Western Studies at Brigham Young University, and from the Honorable John Calhoun Smith Memorial Fund at the University of Idaho, for supporting my original doctoral research.

Finally, this text would have not been possible without the support and understanding of my family. My parents, Ed and Niki Corbin, provided much of the foundation on which this endeavor was placed. My children, Nelson, Anna, and Jack Elam, were always patient with a tedious, and often time-consuming process. My husband, Chip, deserves the greatest thanks of all. His gentle support and guidance are the two things that made a sometimes difficult process seem worthwhile in the greater scheme of our lives together.

Thank you all—Annalies

The Life and Times of the Steamboat *Red Cloud*

or

How Merchants, Mounties, and the Missouri Transformed the West

Introduction

May Flanagan remarked in her personal journal that July 11, 1882, was a notably windy day on the upper Missouri River. She was conscious of such conditions as she hoped for nothing but optimal weather that July. May was a passenger on the steamboat *Red Cloud,* traveling from Bismarck, Dakota Territory, to her home in Fort Benton, Montana Territory. Like so many before her, May and her family were making the long journey on a steamboat. Although highly romanticized, even at the time of May's journey, steamboat travel in the Missouri River West was routine. In fact, travel by river steamer was so commonplace that May recalled most of the men and boys on the boat were enjoying the day despite the wind. Many were up on deck shooting at passing buffalo.[1]

July 11, 1882, it turned out, was a day that May and her fellow passengers would never forget. At nine in the morning, the *Red Cloud* struck a snag, tearing a 40-foot slice in the steamer's side. May recalled that the captain was at the wheel at the time of the incident trying desperately to get the doomed steamer to shore so that none of the passengers were injured. The good captain, according to May, put on full steam and managed to make two lengths of the boat toward shore before striking the sand bar on which the steamer settled 5 feet below the water's surface. The *Red Cloud*'s hold quickly filled with water as the river rushed in. Seven hours later all of the passengers and the deck freight were transferred to another steamboat for the final leg of the journey.[2]

The steamboat *Red Cloud* is central to this story. Its sinking is an important event in the history of both the Missouri River drainage and the American West. The Fort Benton mercantile firm of I. G. Baker & Company owned the *Red Cloud,* the designated flagship of the Baker Line of steamboats. Like the company that owned her, the *Red Cloud* represented business ventures, sustained newly developed and exploited forms of communication and commerce, and contributed to the shaping of the land through which she passed. Yet for all of her success and despite her last unfortunate mishap, the steamboat *Red Cloud* is just another Missouri River steamer. The vessel is important for its representative role in overall American river history and became a time capsule in the study of a common event in the larger narrative of the westward movement.[3]

The *Benton Weekly Record* confirmed that the *Red Cloud* sank within three minutes, after first hitting a snag and then settling on a sandbar a few miles above old Fort Peck, Montana Territory. Although all of the passengers and deck cargo were saved, the boat carried 3,000 bags of flour and other mercantile goods into the mud. Both the cargo and the vessel were reported as a total loss.[4]

The *Red Cloud* highlights the I. G. Baker & Company, tying this narrative of the Missouri River's commercial development with the opening of the Canadian West, including the formation of the Canadian North-West Mounted Police. Each of these ideas on their own represents an individual piece of the greater story of the American-Canadian West, but none of them fully completes the story without the *Red Cloud* as the common denominator. As will be seen, settlement of the borderland West was dependent on the Missouri River as its central supply artery prior to the coming of the railroad. I. G. Baker & Company's steamboat *Red Cloud* fundamentally ties the broader history of the era to one of the region's single most important communities and to the mercantile enterprise in which it flourished.

1

Manifest Destiny and the Missouri River West

May 27, 1880 is a date to be especially remembered
by a number of Montana pioneers, myself among them, for it marked the
arrival of the steamer "Red Cloud" at the Fort Benton levee after a
continuous voyage of seventy-seven days coming
upriver from St. Louis.

—Lou Stocking Stewart, remembrance, 1937

Movement west was manifest since the beginning of the European incursion on the Atlantic coast. An apparently empty North American continent drew in new inhabitants. Since the founding of Jamestown, Euroamericans moved toward the Pacific Ocean. By the mid-nineteenth century, American expansion westward across the continent was more than just wanderlust, many at the time considered it a God-given right.

In this light, the steamboat *Red Cloud* becomes the embodiment of one of America's greatest nineteenth-century aspirations—the need, drive, and desire to grow and expand beyond its settled regions. The *Red Cloud* is a metaphor for nineteenth-century American passion, not only to control but to conquer; through both will and technology Americans deemed themselves destined to control an entire continent. New York journalist John O'Sullivan argued most fervently for the divine right of expansion. In 1839 he called the United States a nation *destined to manifest;* in 1845 he finally arrived at the enduring slogan, *manifest destiny.* O'Sullivan argued, "the nation of many nations is destined to manifest to mankind the excellence of divine principles; to establish on earth the noblest temple ever dedicated to the worship of the Most High—the Sacred and the True."[1]

Figure 1.1. The steamboat *Red Cloud* on the Missouri River, n.d. Murphy Library, University of Wisconsin–La Crosse (photograph no. 40635).

Historians Julius Pratt and Frederick Merk later suggested that O'Sullivan had, in fact, captured the essence of a growing American feeling. O'Sullivan's term, *manifest destiny,* identified the nation's increasing desire to push for expansion over an area not yet defined, although prearranged by heaven. "It was our nation's obvious fate to expand from sea to sea."[2] By the 1840s, O'Sullivan's vision of expansion was more than just a possibility. It was, in fact, a reality. The past obstacles to growth that prevented a single United States, stretching from the Atlantic to the Pacific, were now gone. The physical means of transport were available by the 1840s, and the nation's surging population would allow the immigration to and conquest of the vast West. Early American westward movement was directly dependent on the opening of the Mississippi drainage. The Mississippi's primary tributary, the Missouri River, quickly became the gateway to the West.

Whether moving inward from the Atlantic coast or through the Ohio and Mississippi valleys, it was by way of the nation's extensive inland river system that Euroamericans first moved west. The rivers were not only the first and most extensive passage into the interior but also the most enduring

Map 1.1. The Missouri River Basin. Drawn by Jack Scott, 1999.

highway until the turn of the twentieth century. United States' *manifest destiny* both followed and flowed through the nation's rivers. The key to gaining access to the deepest parts of the interior of North America was to understand and ultimately to conquer the Mississippi-Missouri River system.

The first reported Euroamericans to see the Missouri River were Father Jacquets Marquette and his companion Louis Joliet in June 1673.[3] They knew the river as the "Pekitanoui" from a local Indian. In a small birch-bark canoe, the pair paddled down the Mississippi toward the mouth of the Missouri River. What Marquette saw both surprised and appalled him. He reported that the crashing noise of rapids heralded the transition from the clear Mississippi River to its violent collision with the Pekitanoui (Missouri):

> As we were gently sail[ed] down the still clear water, we hear[d] a noise of a rapid[s] into which we were about to fall. I have seen nothing more frightful, a mass of large trees entire with branches, real floating Islands came from Pekitanoui, so impetuous that we could not without great danger expose ourselves to pass across. The agitation was so great that the water was all muddy, and could not get clear. The Pekitanoui is a considerable river coming from the northwest and empties into the Mississippi. Many towns are located on this river and I hope by it to make the discovery of the Vermillion or California sea.[4]

Most of those who followed the path first taken by Father Marquette noted the turbulence and violence of the Missouri River. It simultaneously created and destroyed the land through which it passed. The Missouri River, however, was the eastern gateway to the American West; it was the most direct route to the land, resources, and people that lay beyond the settled regions of the Mississippi Valley and the eastern seaboard. To achieve *manifest destiny* and spread from ocean to ocean, Americans had to tame and, in turn, be molded by the great Missouri River.

Whether set up as centers of trade with Native Americans during the fur trade era or as distribution points for mining activity, the first western communities sprang up along rivers. Euroamerican interlopers quickly adopted Native American canoes and bullboats for use on the river. Mackinaws and keelboats soon followed. The great breakthrough, and the key to the opening of the American West, came when steamboats were introduced on the Mississippi and Missouri rivers. The capacity and speed they brought allowed for the necessary people, goods, and ideas that ultimately shaped a vast American frontier.[5] The steamboat era, although relatively short, was a pivotal period in the history of the United States because it changed all aspects of life along the river.

So profound was the long-term impact of steamboat operations on the Missouri River that historian Hiram Chittenden argued, in 1902, "it seldom happened that the introduction of labor-saving devices has not robbed society to some extent of what was poetic and sentimental, and replaced it by something more prosaic and matter of fact. The Missouri River steamboat was an exception."[6] By the turn of the twentieth century, volumes of highly romanticized history were written about the glory of the fur trade era (1808 through the mid-1840s) and the Missouri River keelboats that accompanied it. Chittenden suggested that the history of the steamboat was far more romantic. How could one not be moved by the sight of "one of these noble vessels, standing high above the water line and well above the highest banks, its white form sharply outlined against the foliage of the bottoms, its lofty chimneys pouring out clouds of smoke, its apparent ease in stemming the swift current?"[7]

Steamboats operating along the Missouri River had long-term impact upon life in the region. To the native populations the boats were viewed as strange and somewhat supernatural. The steamers first transported the men and supplies of the fur trade but later were an integral part of all commerce, public or private, along the river. As a result, Chittenden's notion that "no feature of frontier life is more intimately blended with the history of the Western country than the Missouri River steamboat" was well placed.[8]

Figure 1.2. The steamboat *De Smet* and cargo at the Fort Benton levee, ca. 1870. Montana Historical Society, Helena (photograph no. 955-110).

For three decades, from1860 through 1890, steamboat travel on the upper Missouri (the region of the river above Council Bluffs, Iowa) defined the westward progression of settlement and followed a seasonal rhythm. Spring came, not when the ice broke, but when the season's first shipment of supplies arrived at the levee. A steamboat's arrival often meant new furniture, new striped stockings, and perhaps a new hat style from the east, or maybe even oranges or grapes. Many residents of remote steamboat towns would long remember that, as children, they found it remarkable to discover that apples and corn were not just dried or canned but could be fresh if delivered by steamboat. So striking were those events that residents remembered their families calling the steamboat fare "skin apples" and "stick corn."[9]

The veritable assortment of treasures off-loaded on the levee would often include stoves, barrels of flour and whisky, buggies, chickens, and hair-footed Clydesdale horses, to name just a few. The streets of the western steamboat towns would bustle with the ox and mule trains loading from the waterfront warehouses to take goods, both novel and practical, to surrounding towns.[10] Life for many on the frontier depended on the yearly arrival of supplies, immigrants, mail, and long-absent family—all carried upriver by steamboat. Consequently, the loss of steamers to accidents meant hardship for the same communities that celebrated successful arrivals. The 1882 loss of the *Red Cloud* was just such an instance. Ultimately, this wreck cost the community of Fort Benton, Montana, more than just the flour she carried in her hold.

The sinking of the *Red Cloud* came on the eve of a great change on the high plains. Commerce, previously dependent strictly on the river, was slowly waning as the number of railroad lines increased in the region. Towns once linked to the commerce of the east by an extensive and complex system of steamboat and adjoining wagon roads were now linked by the railroad. As river communities like Fort Benton were by-passed by the rail lines, they slowly died while new communities far from navigable waterways began to flourish. The life and times of the high plains was changing and so was the importance of steamboating on the Missouri River.

2

Claiming the Missouri River: The Evolution of the Steamboat Eras

> The passengers were a fine class of people, many of them on their first trip up river and determined to make a success of western life. They were not adventurers, but homeseekers who later located throughout northern Montana.
>
> —Lou Stocking Stewart, remembrance, 1937

President Thomas Jefferson sent Meriwether Lewis and William Clark's Corps of Discovery, the first organized exploration by Americans, up the Missouri River in 1804. Long before Lewis and Clark returned to St. Louis in 1806, however, the Missouri River was already recognized as the gateway to the nation's deepest interior. The French established the first permanent European post on the Missouri River in 1722, when they settled Fort Orleans about 250 miles above the mouth of the river.[1] In 1807, St. Louis merchant and fur trader, Manuel Lisa, established the first American upper river fur trade post on the banks of the Missouri's Big Horn River in what would become Montana Territory.[2] The organized development of the American West was underway.

Fur traders led the march in exploiting the Missouri River. British, French Canadian, Spanish, and American trappers and traders flocked to the pelt-rich Missouri River valley. Well through the 1820s and 1830s, small boats traveled the Missouri River system carrying the annual provisions from the supply houses in St. Louis and returning with the year's catch of furs. At the outset, Native American bullboats (washtub-shaped boats, made by both trappers and Indians, that had stretched wet buffalo hides over a willow frame) proved most versatile.[3] Canoes and mackinaws were also put into service. Mackinaws were flat-bottomed boats of extremely light draft that only came into being on the Missouri River after the establishment of upriver sawmills. Although unable to buck strong currents going upriver, the mackinaw had advantages over the bullboat and the canoe due to its flat bottom, sharp prow, and rudder that allowed it to avoid obstacles while traveling downstream.[4]

By far, the most popular small boat before the appearance of steamboats was the keelboat. Keelboats ranged in length from 40 feet to 80 feet with a shallow keel and a defined "point" at both ends. These versatile boats usually carried between 15 and 30 tons of freight, including men, supplies, and furs, along the river. It was the swarthy St. Louis fur trader, Manuel Lisa, who really introduced the sustained use of keelboats on the Missouri. Lisa had a keelboat specially built for the shallows and obstacles of the Missouri. His boat was so successful that other fur traders quickly adopted his design.[5]

The fur trade ultimately drove the need to bring steamboats to the Missouri River. The wealth in the fur trade, often referred to as the lure for "soft gold" by modern historians, was enormous. The riches of the trade made men, like the American Fur Company's John Jacob Astor, kings of a vast empire by the mid-1830s.[6] By this time the steamboat was quickly becoming the craft of preference for the lower river. After the fur trade, military operations, mining in the Rockies and Montana, and settlement in the various upper Plains regions along the river fueled an increase in steamboat traffic on the Missouri.

Steamboats on the Missouri River: The Fur Trade Era

The first steamer reached St. Louis on the Mississippi in 1817 and many traders, trappers, and merchants quickly began one of the region's greatest debates: Can steamboats navigate the Missouri River? The debate ran long and hard. Despite the great success of early steamboating on the Ohio and Mississippi rivers, many questioned whether the Missouri River was navigable by steamboat at all. Historian Stanley Vestal suggested that the argument must have raged in every river community at least once a day until the matter was emphatically settled through repeated, successful trips by steamboats up the Missouri.[7]

The St. Louis resident, George Fitch, argued at the time that the Missouri was indeed navigable; the problem was that, "those who have tried it have spent too much time trying to change the river to conform to the steamboats when they should have been making over the steamboats to conform to the river."[8] He suggested a redesign of the steamboat to solve the problem. A Missouri River steamer had to be shallow, lithe, deep-chested, and strong in the stern wheel. Fitch argued that, in addition to those basic design elements, the steamers should be hinged in the middle and fitted with a suction dredge so that all sand bars proving impassable could simply be assimilated. He warned that a Missouri River steamer should be able to make use of an open channel but should not be dependent on one. After all, a steamer that "cannot, on occasion, climb a steep clay bank, go across a cornfield and corner a river that is trying to get away, has little excuse for trying to navigate the Missouri."[9] Fitch had a point. Few who lived along the banks of the Missouri failed to recognize that the Missouri was a cantankerous river, a river that was hard enough to manage in a keelboat, let alone a steamer.

Steamboating on the Missouri River began in May 1819 when Colonel Elias Rector decided to take the challenge. Colonel Rector established a steamboat company for the sole purpose of seeing whether or not the Missouri was indeed navigable. On May 28, 1819, Rector's 98-ton *Independence* ascended 250 miles above St. Louis, arriving at Franklin, Missouri. The arrival was heralded as "no ordinary sensations of pride and pleasure," by the *Missouri Intelligencer* as not only the first steamboat ever to attempt to navigate the Missouri but for also conveying passengers, flour, whiskey, sugar, iron, and more.[10] The steamer then proceeded beyond Franklin to its final destination of Chariton, Missouri. Both towns celebrated the arrival of the boat as the "proudest event in the history of the Missouri."[11] The town of Franklin held a dinner party in honor of the event, in which no fewer than twenty-three toasts were made.

Major Steven H. Long of the Corps of Topographical Engineers also traveled up the Missouri by steamboat in 1819, as part of the U.S. government's Yellowstone Expedition.[12] The principal objective of Yellowstone Expedition was to construct posts at the Mandan villages and at the mouth of the Yellowstone River. The posts were proposed as a barrier to British incursion into American territory. Long's steamer, the *Western Engineer*, and three other steamers were to transport troops and military supplies as far as Fort Lisa, a small trading post a few miles above present-day Omaha.

Making it to Fort Lisa was not a simple task for the steamboats involved. Three of the steamboats used on the expedition, the *R. M. Johnson*, the *Expedition*, and the *Thomas Jefferson*, were supplied by a private contractor, James Johnson of Kentucky. Built for use on the Ohio River, Johnson's boats fared worse than the purpose-built *Western Engineer* in the extreme shallows of the Missouri. Due to low water, the *R. M. Johnson* only

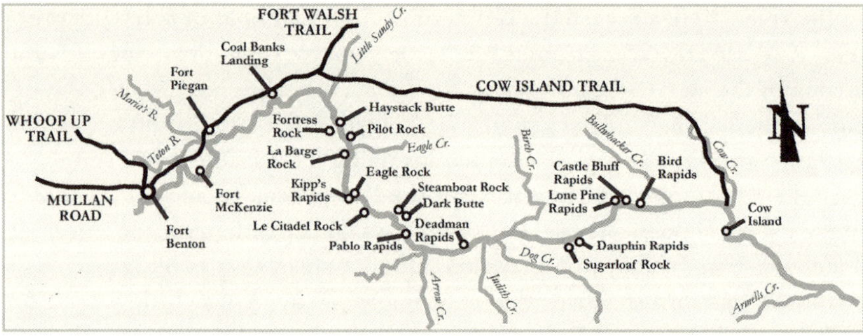

Map 2.1. Locations of steamboat landings, island, bends, and such on the Missouri River in the nineteenth century. Drawn by Nathan Richards, 2004.

reached a point between Fort Osage and Cow Island; the *Expedition* went aground near Cow Island; and the *Jefferson* broke a piston, making it only as far as the mouth of the Osage River. A fourth boat, the *Calhoun,* was scheduled to participate but never made it to the Missouri River.[13] Long's flagship, the *Western Engineer,* not only made the entire journey but did so in style. The bow of the steamer resembled the head of a serpent and had the smokestack discharging out of the serpent's mouth. The steamer was affectionately called "Long's Dragon" and was intended to intimidate the Indians.[14] With Long's 1819 success it finally seemed that there would be no stopping the progress of steamboats up the Missouri.

Despite such grand beginnings, the succeeding decades of the 1820s and 1830s were a lackluster time for steamboating on the lower Missouri River (the 660 miles between St. Louis and Council Bluffs). Few boats were put in operation; the journey proved both dangerous and arduous; and the schedules of the boats that did operate were irregular at best, due to a lack of settlement and limited commerce along the river.[15] Yet immigration insured that commerce gradually increased. The first regular steam packet (combination freight and passenger haulers) service running from St. Louis to Independence began in 1829; service to Westport and St. Joseph soon followed. By 1831, five regular packets ran on the Lower Missouri; by 1836, fifteen to twenty made regular round trips to Boonville and Glasgow. In 1842, thirty-six boats operated on the lower river.[16]

The signature event in upper Missouri River steamboating came in 1831, when the Western Department of the American Fur Company's steamboat, the *Yellow Stone,*[17] ascended the Missouri River as far as Fort Tecumseh, present-day Pierre, South Dakota.[18] The next year the vessel reached Kenneth McKenzie's Fort Union, Dakota Territory, the staging post for expansion into the northern Plains and Rockies, at the mouth of the Yellowstone River, a grueling distance of 1,300 miles.[19] After exchanging her cargo of supplies for furs and pelts, the *Yellow Stone* returned to St. Louis, proving finally that the "grand experiment" of steamboating on the Missouri River was more than just a dream.

The American Fur Company quickly capitalized on the success of the *Yellow Stone* when, in 1833, the Company's second steamer, the *Assiniboine,*[20] arrived at Fort Union carrying Prince Maximilian and artist Charles Bodmer on their famous and well-chronicled exploration of the Missouri.[21] The success of the *Yellow Stone* and the *Assiniboine* drove the Company to experiment with more boats, and the firm successfully dispatched one or more boats upriver every season until the company sold its operations in 1864.[22]

Reaching Fort Union was a notable achievement, and for many years there was little need to push upriver from the great fur Mecca of the high plains. As the years passed, however, and as the American Fur Company's enterprises developed further upriver, the need for steamboats beyond Fort Union increased.[23] In 1834, John Jacob Astor sold his interest in the

Figure 2.1. The American Fur Company's steamboat, *Yellow Stone.* Fort Union National Historic Landmark, National Park Service.

Figure 2.2. Fort Benton, Montana, as drawn in ca. 1869.

American Fur Company to Bernard Pratte Sr. and Pierre Chouteau Jr., both of whom had been active in Company activities. The pair operated the company from 1834 through 1838 as Pratte, Chouteau, & Company. In 1838, sole control of the company passed to Pierre Chouteau Jr., who reorganized the firm as Pierre Chouteau Jr. & Company. Although officially reorganized as Pierre Chouteau Jr. & Company, the firm continued to be commonly known as the American Fur Company until it was disbanded in 1865, and often appears that way in the literature.

In 1847, the Company established Fort Benton (called Fort Lewis until 1850) on the north shore of the far upper Missouri River in Montana Territory. Created as the company's northernmost Missouri River post, Fort Benton was strategically placed approximately 2,500 miles above St. Louis, and 500 miles from Fort Union, the central depot of the American Fur Company. The first few years of Fort Benton's history were rather unremarkable. Conflicts with the Indians restricted activities at the post and Fort Union was still considered more important. Beginning in 1853, however, the status of Fort Benton began to change as government interest in the region increased.

Placing Fort Benton on the National Map

In 1853, the U.S. government sent Isaac Ingalls Stevens overland from St. Paul, Minnesota, to assume the office of Territorial Governor of Washington and to survey a proposed railroad route to Puget Sound via Fort Ben-

Joel F. Overholser Historical Research Center, Schwinden Library and Archives, Fort Benton, Montana (photograph no. 95-RP-022-M).

ton. Accompanying Stevens was an enthusiastic young West Point graduate, Lieutenant John Mullan. While Stevens traveled overland to Fort Union at the mouth of the Yellowstone River, Mullan headed the survey party that traveled up the Missouri River on the steamboat *Robert Campbell.*[24] The original plan was for Stevens and Mullan to rendezvous at Fort Union and then to travel together to Fort Benton by steamboat. Low water and the hazards of the Missouri River greatly hampered the expedition's progress. Managing only 75 miles above Fort Union by steamboat, the group finally reached Fort Benton through a combination of overland travel and keelboat transport. A rigorous journey, no doubt, but one that highlighted the importance of pushing steamboat navigation to Fort Benton.[25]

After their arrival at Fort Benton, Stevens pushed west to assume his new office and to continue his exploration of the northern Rockies and Cascade ranges. Stevens was certain that a practical northern railroad route to the Pacific was possible. To that end, Stevens left Lieutenant Mullan and thirteen men at Fort Owen, an outpost on the upper reaches of Clarks Fork and the Coeur d'Alene Mountains, to collect winter weather data in the region of the proposed rail route. Although the general purpose of the survey was to find a suitable route for the railroad, historian Oscar Winther argues that it was clear from the outset that Mullan "sensed the more immediate prospect of constructing over the mountains a wagon road which [would] join together the two great river basins of the Columbia and the Missouri."[26] So certain was Mullan of the usability of a wagon road in the region that he formally suggested that the road be considered in his official report of his winter explorations. In 1854, when Mullan returned east, he found that Congress had appropriated $30,000 for a survey of a military road between Fort Benton, on the Missouri River, and Wallula (old Fort Walla Walla) on the Columbia River. Mullan was asked to take charge of the work.[27]

The long-term potential of such a road could not be denied. If successfully completed, the proposed road would make it possible for immigrants, military, and commercial goods to ship from St. Louis up the Missouri River to Fort Benton, across the new military road, and then either overland via the existing wagon roads from Wallula or by vessel down the Columbia River all the way to the Pacific coast. Despite the obvious advantages of such a road, the project was plagued by bureaucratic setbacks. It was 1858 before Mullan was granted official notice to begin the survey. Once underway, obstacles hampered the survey, the most significant being that the Palouse Indians were on the warpath and looking to stop Mullan's survey party. The ensuing conflict put off Mullan's project until June of 1859.

The delay was not without its advantages, however. During the Indian conflict, Congress decided that the proposed military road was desperately needed to maintain the peace in the area. As a result, Congress appropriated an additional $100,000, not only for the survey but also for the actual construction of the Fort Benton–Wallula Road. On June 4, 1859, Mullan and his construction crew finally began the tedious task of constructing what came to be known as the Mullan Road. Beginning at the mouth of the Palouse River, Mullan's crew worked in a northerly direction until they reached the St. Regis Borgia Valley where the men spent the winter of 1859.[28]

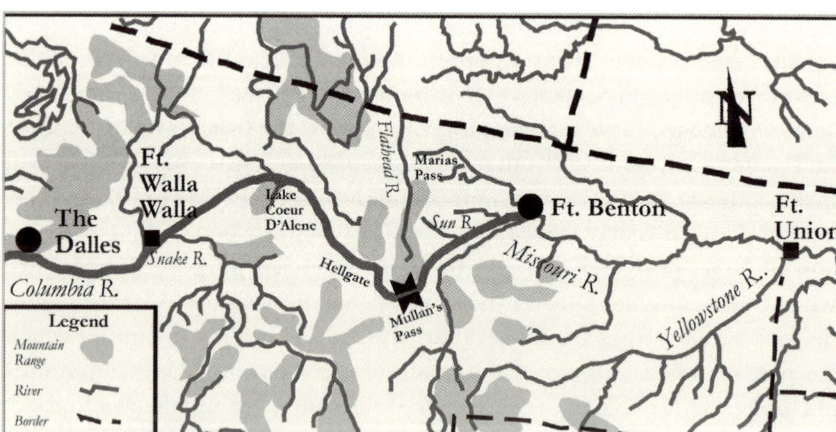

Map 2.2. The Mullan Road. Drawn by Nathan Richards, 2004.

Work the following spring of 1860 was strenuous as the crew completed one of the most difficult sections of the road. The area, near present-day Missoula, Montana, took 150 men six weeks to cut a road through a 6-mile section of rugged land. On August 5, 1860, the work was finally completed when Mullan and his crew reached Fort Benton. Upon his arrival Mullan found Major Blake and three hundred troops awaiting transport over the new road to garrisons in Washington and eastern Oregon. While Blake and his men prepared for the next leg of their journey, Mullan returned over the newly completed road. Along the way Mullan's crew constantly improved the road in advance of the troops. Blake and his men quickly followed, making the 624-mile trek in a record fifty-seven days. Not only were the troops the first official contingent to use the new road, but it was estimated that the transport of troops over the new road saved the government $30,000 over transportation costs along an alternate route.[29]

As a military highway, the road was relatively unimportant in the long run, and there was little large-scale military use of the road after Blake's initial march. In many places the route was little more than a pack trail, and the road was never deemed fit for continuous wagon traffic. Despite these drawbacks, the road was crucial to early settlement in Montana since it connected the gold fields of Idaho and the Columbia River and linked Fort Benton to the growing extraction industries in the South and West.[30]

Fort Benton's status was further improved in 1855 when the government concluded a treaty with the Blackfeet and Flathead Indians as a first step in safeguarding further exploration and surveying in the upper river region. The Blackfeet and Flathead treaties were crucial in opening trade opportunities for civilian supply contractors on both sides of the Continental Divide. Pierre Chouteau Jr. would naturally want to exploit the lower transportation costs of taking goods as far as possible via the Missouri River. Lower costs would be necessary if Chouteau and his Missouri River enterprise hoped to survive once Portland and the Mullan overland route was completed. Chouteau obtained the supply contracts for the various Mullan expeditions and recognized that ultimately the success of the Mullan road as an immigrant and military route to the Columbia River country would still require regular steamboat traffic from St. Louis to Fort Benton, thereby allowing his company to remain active in the region.[31]

The government's interest and foothold in the region was further solidified in 1859 when the Raynolds Expedition set out to map the Missouri River region. Once again, Chouteau found himself heavily involved in the government's next big activity in the region. Major W. F. Raynolds was ordered to explore the "mountain region about the sources of the Yellowstone and Missouri, to ascertain the character of the routes leading south and west from the navigable parts of those rivers."[32] The emphasis of the Raynolds expedition was to encourage both commercial and settlement development of the upper Missouri and Yellowstone drainage area. It was hoped that the preliminary geographical study would be of use to traders, settlers, and future military endeavors. Pierre Chouteau Jr. secured the contract to transport Raynolds and his survey party up the Missouri River. Historian William Lass appropriately suggested that it was the combination of the surge in government activity, along with the Chouteau's trading activity in the Fort Benton area, that led to the "final conquest of the Missouri," through the use of steamboats.[33]

Crucial to Chouteau's surge in business was his use of his connections inside the federal government. In 1855, Chouteau had won an exclusive government contract to deliver the annuity goods promised in the Blackfeet treaty. The lure of potential profits from government contracts only fueled the company's desire for steamboats to navigate all the way to Fort Benton, thus cutting out the expensive mackinaw or overland freighting costs from Fort Union.[34] Almost three decades after the initial success of the *Yellow Stone,*[35] Chouteau and Company built the steamboat *Chippewa* in 1857 for use in fulfilling the government contracts Chouteau had acquired.[36] The *Chippewa* was a light draft boat with high pressure engines designed for the shallow waters of the far upper Missouri River.

The new steamer and its companion vessel, the *Spread Eagle,* left St. Louis on the May 28, 1859.[37] The steamboats and their crews met Raynolds and his outfit upriver, at St. Joseph, on the 4th of June. When the steamers left St. Joseph, they were heavily loaded with the annual supplies for the company, annuities for the upper Missouri and Blackfoot agencies, goods for the Teton Sioux at Fort Pierre, supplies for Mullan's road project, and Raynolds's complete outfitting needs (animals, provisions, and camp equipment). Raynolds's party disembarked from the steamers at Fort Pierre and then headed overland to Fort Sarpy on the Yellowstone River. The *Spread Eagle* and *Chippewa* continued upriver to Fort Union where Raynolds's supplies were off-loaded and stored.

Accompanying the steamers on this voyage was Pierre Chouteau Jr.'s son, Charles P. Chouteau. Charles was assigned the task of encouraging the steamboat captains to try traveling farther upriver toward Fort Benton, if the river conditions made this possible. Charles made his attempt in the smaller, purpose-built *Chippewa.* Under his guidance, the boat managed to steam within walking distance of Fort Benton, Montana Territory, the effective head of steamboat navigation on the Missouri River.[38]

The following year, the spring of 1860, Chouteau and Company's two steamers, the *Chippewa* and the newly built *Key West,* churned up the Missouri again, this time tying up at Fort Benton.[39] The *Chippewa* offloaded 250 tons of cargo.[40] This trip set a new distance record in the history of steamboat navigation and established Fort Benton as the steamboat capital of the upper northwest region.[41]

Gold Rush in the Mountains: Montana Territory Comes of Age

By the time Pierre Chouteau Jr. had successfully established Fort Benton as the terminus of steamboat navigation on the Missouri, Montana was on the verge of great change. Although the fur trade was still prominent in the region as a whole, by the mid-1850s the trade was changing. Beaver pelts were no longer the driving force; the species had been heavily trapped and the trade was shifting toward hides. Profits were not what they were in the 1830s. The gold rush soon eclipsed fur as the primary economic force in Montana.[42]

Historian Oscar Winther argued that the period 1857 through 1865 defined Montana's first great moment in history. The gold diggings were the driving force that brought Montana territorial status on May 26, 1864. Gold was first found in Montana in 1852, but prospecting was not taken seriously in the area until the 1857–58 arrival of Granville Stuart, who helped publicize the gold fields back East. Over time, word spread that gold had been discovered in the Idaho and Montana region. Finally, gold fever struck the region with the 1862–64 discovery of rich placer and quartz mines at Gold Creek, Bannack, Alder Gulch, Deer Lodge, Last Chance Gulch (Helena), and Virginia City.[43]

With the discovery of the placer mines in 1862 came a surge of miners and speculators to an area with relatively few white inhabitants. The rapid influx of people was simply overwhelming. By 1863 Virginia City had 3,450 residents and Nevada City housed another 3,075 individuals. There were a reported 11,493 people by 1864 in Madison County, home of Alder Gulch, and the total population of the Territory was a remarkable 15,822. Within two years, the region that was once called home by Indians, trappers, traders, and a few farmers now had a population sufficient to apply for territorial admission. In response, the Territory of Montana was created on May 26, 1864.[44]

The sudden increase in population put new strains on the region that directly affected the development of commerce and transportation. The pre-gold population of traders, trappers, and farmers could live off the land; the miners could not. The mining population was almost entirely dependent on outside resources for food, clothing, and the tools of the trade. Almost all of these goods had to be brought across significant distances from outside the immediate region. Bannock and Virginia City were 400 miles from Salt Lake City, 1,400 miles from Omaha, 1,000 miles from Portland, 600 miles from the head of navigation on the Columbia River, and 200 miles from Fort Benton.[45]

In one form or another, each of those commercial centers was vying for the new Montana trade. By 1865, supplies were shuttled to the mining camps of Montana by three primary routes: supplies came overland from the East to Salt Lake City and then north by wagon; from Portland and Walla Walla via the Mullan Road; and from St. Louis to Fort Benton via the Missouri River. Of the three primary transportation routes into Montana in use in 1865, it was the Montana Trail (Salt Lake City—later Corinne—to Fort Benton), that would compete most successfully with the Missouri River route for trade.

The Montana Trail stretched 625 miles from Salt Lake City to Fort Benton. The trail came into prominence with the July 1862 establishment of gold diggings at Grasshopper Creek in western Montana. Miners rushed to what would become Bannock City from all over the West. Some seventy-five miners were at work in the area in 1862, with another three hundred soon to arrive. The sudden surge of miners around Grasshopper Creek, most without yearly supplies, created opportunity for freighters in Salt Lake City. By 1864, the use of the overland Montana Trail was firmly established with the big strike at Last Chance Gulch. Until the completion of the transcontinental railroad in 1869, Salt Lake City would serve as one of the main supply depots in the West. With the increased needs in Montana, several large-scale professional freighters entered the northern trade. These freighters carried mining machinery and other bulk goods. Joining the freighters were a number of the region's farmers, who profited from the new markets Montana offered for their produce. Even with an increase in Montana farm production, fruit and flour from the rich farmland of Utah would always find ready markets in western Montana.[46]

Competing with Salt Lake City and the Montana Trail freighters were the West Coast suppliers and pack-train operators. The pack-train operators were experienced because they had been freighting into the Idaho mining regions since the first big gold rush in 1860. Walla Walla, the eastern terminus of Columbia River steamboating, had quickly become the distributing center for mining and related activities throughout much of the northwest, particularly in the Salmon River, Boise Basin, the Owyhee mines

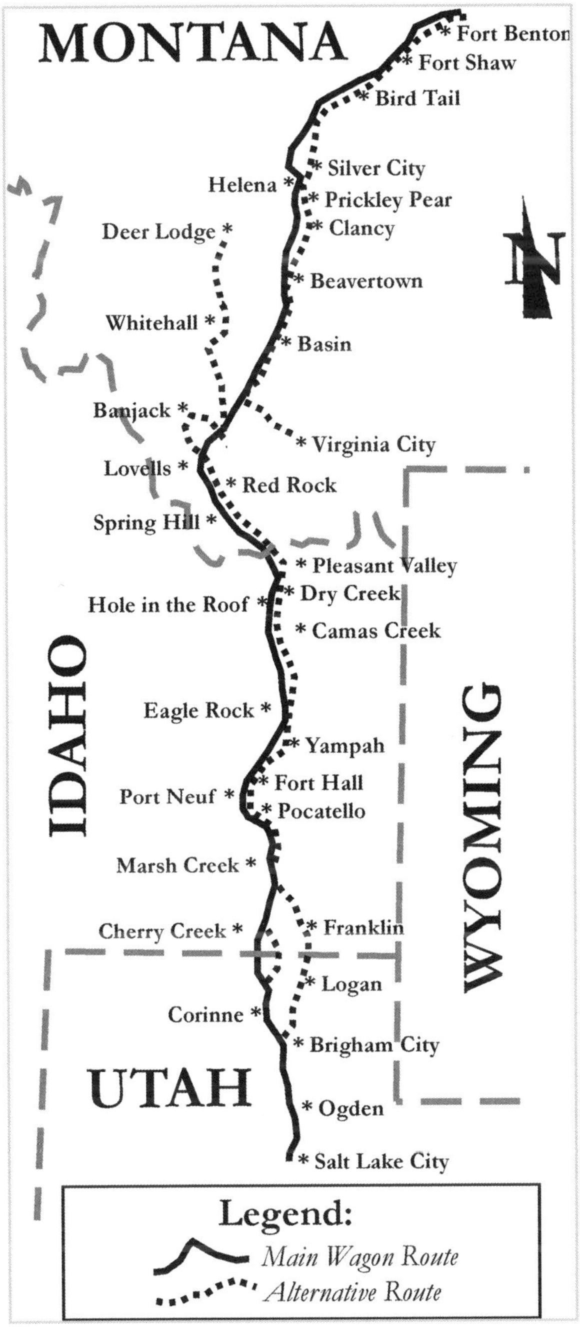

Map 2.3. The Montana Trail. Drawn by Nathan Richards, 2004.

in Idaho, and the mines on the Powder and John Day rivers in Oregon. Several trails radiated from the bustling little community of Walla Walla, and, when the mining frontier opened up to the east, the packers simply followed the swell of miners headed into Montana. The pack-trains from Oregon and Washington supplied some of the first bacon, beans, flour, clothing, and mining supplies in the Bannock, Alder Gulch, and Last Chance mining districts.[47]

The most popular route from Walla Walla to Montana was the newly completed Mullan Road. Although the route never saw significant military use, the road was irreplaceable as an immigrant and supply route into western Montana. The picks and shovels used in the first serious mining operation in Montana came via the Mullan Road, as did the supplies used to open the first store in Hell Gate, Montana. By the spring of 1864, pack-trains were a regular sight on the Mullan Road. Few wagons actually traveled the Mullan Road, despite Mullan's vision, and the road was rarely maintained well enough for large freight wagons. The majority of the freight that passed along the Mullan route did so on the back of mules. The freight-hauling mule trains became so prevalent that it was not unusual for five trains a day to be reported passing through Hell Gate in the summer of 1864. By 1865, Portland merchants were busy shipping supplies to Walla Walla for further shipment into the markets of western Montana. Complex commercial and freighting networks sprang up as West Coast merchants looked to cut into the profits of the Salt Lake City capitalists. The result was a lively and competitive trade for several years.[48]

The steamboat supply line through Fort Benton became another important competitor for the region's mining-inspired business. Despite Chouteau's efforts between 1860 and 1864, no more than four steamers arrived at Fort Benton in any one season; the fur trade alone did not provide enough financial opportunities to compel many steamboat owners and operators to risk their vessels on the precarious conditions of the upper Missouri. The potential profits of the Montana gold rush after 1858, however, shifted the tempo of upper river steamboating. In 1865, Fort Benton had eight steamboats tie up at the levee, thirty-one in 1866, thirty-nine in 1868, and twenty-four in 1869. It was not uncommon by the end of the decade for as many as seven steamers to unload at the Fort Benton levee at the same time.[49]

Once the Montana mining boom was underway, St. Louis merchants quickly began forming mining and transportation companies with the aim of supplying the Argonauts via Fort Benton. Early efforts in St Louis were slowed somewhat during General Alfred Sully's Sioux Indian campaigns (1863–64) in the Missouri River region. Sully's expedition did, nonetheless, have long-range impact on Missouri River steamboating. First and foremost, Sully's enterprise demonstrated the versatility of steamboats on the Missouri. His two-year effort made use of fifteen different steamers for supply, two of which became the first steamboats ever to navigate the Yellowstone River. Next, during his push, Sully established two new Missouri River military posts, Fort Sully near present-day Pierre and Fort Rice below Bismarck. Both posts were best supplied by St. Louis–based steamboats.[50]

Missouri River freighting between 1860 and 1865 was further slowed by periods of chronic drought and continuing hostilities with the Teton Sioux, but in the first few years of Fort Benton–bound steamboating, St. Louis merchants laid a solid foundation for upper river shipping in the gold rush years to come. The return of high water and the expansion of mining in Montana finally brought upper Missouri River steamboating into its own in 1865.[51]

In the four years from 1866 to 1869, local Fort Benton historian Joel Overholser estimated that no fewer than 150 steamboats arrived at Fort Benton. With the vessels came the "mining machinery and food supplies for the luxury-hungry miners of the isolated mines at Bannock, Virginia City, Helena, and Butte."[52] The lure of gold was without a doubt the driving force for the whole region. Where the early fur trade pulled in the barons of St. Louis and a rough assortment of independent traders and mountain men, the quest for hard gold drew people from all walks of life. By 1865, farmers were leaving their families behind and their fields unplowed in places like Iowa and Missouri. Many chased the dream of gold somewhere in Idaho or Montana.

William Wheatley of Missouri was one such man. In 1865, he and a friend booked passage on the ill-fated steamboat *Bertrand* with a sawmill they hoped would help them make a fortune by selling lumber to miners in the Helena goldfields. It took Wheatley six different steamboats and the loading and unloading of his mill seventeen times before he reached Montana—far too late to make a profit with his mill for the season. Despite his personal setbacks, Wheatley experienced the lure of gold first hand. Writing home to his father in 1866, he described the amazing sight of Helena, Montana:

> Helena is a fair specimen of a gold city, and outbangs anything I ever saw or heard of. The main gulch was discovered during the winter of '64 & [6]5 and by April there was a population of 12,000 souls. The city contains large stores in which you can buy anything you want, and that of the

Figure 2.3. The steamboat *Bertrand* as illustrated by Jerry Livingston. Courtesy of the U.S. Fish and Wildlife Service, DeSoto National Wildlife Refuge, Steamboat Bertrand Collection.

> very best quality. There are no poor trifling goods brought to this country. There are livery stables, hotels, theaters, dance houses and all the outfit of an eastern city. The saloons and gambling houses are the finest. I am sorry to say that I found everything but schools and churches.[53]

Even though Wheatley went to Montana to get rich using his mill, he did find that there were more numerous opportunities for making money by digging gold.

At one point, a miner offered to sell Wheatley his claim in Montana Gulch for $100. Wheatley declined the offer, hoping to make it as a merchant instead, perhaps regretting his choice later. He reported that the very same miner returned the next day, after working the claim, with $100,000 in gold dust. Wheatley told his awed father that, "I saw him dig out 6 ft. square [cubic] and wash out $3,300 and this did not take him a whole day. I have seen the nuggets in his gold pan like kernels of walnuts."[54] The same wealth that Wheatley saw first hand in the gold laden gulches was the new driving force on the river.

Supplying the mines and the miners was big business in the 1860s. The potential for profit was enormous both upbound and downbound. Joseph LaBarge, a long-time steamboat captain, estimated that approximately 1,000 passengers and 6,000 tons of freight traveled up the Missouri in 1865. The following year, thirty-one boats arrived at Fort Benton and discharged 4,686 tons of freight.[55] The steamer *Peter Balen* alone brought 400 tons of freight to Fort Benton, in 1866, at 12 1/2 cents a pound for a freight bill worth $100,000.[56]

Few of the miners and speculators actually stayed in Montana and Idaho for very long. As the river freighting season drew to its close, the downbound passenger and freight manifests of the steamers increased. Back downriver went the hundreds who made their strikes for the year, as well as tons of gold dust. On one return trip downriver, in 1866, the *Luella* carried 230 passengers and 2.5 tons of gold dust worth $1.2 million. 1867 was a profitable year as well, with thirty-nine boats docking at Fort Benton. Some of these boats carried back downriver remarkable quantities of gold for a single season. The *Miner* carried $35,000 in gold; the *Only Chance* carried down a reported $500,000 in dust; while the *Cora* transported $100,000, and the *Gallatin* another $250,000.[57]

It was not just steamboating that was successful as a result of the mines. Overland transportation was also booming in conjunction with steamboating. In 1866 alone, an estimated 2,500 men and 3,000 ox and mule teams transported goods from Fort Benton to the various mines of the region for freighters including the Montana & Idaho Transportation Line, J. J. Roe & Co., J. T. Murphy, and King and Gillette.[58]

St. Louis–based steamboating added to the commercial diversity developing in Fort Benton, and ultimately the steamboatmen dominated the Montana trade. The river route proved more cost effective than either the Salt Lake City–Montana Trail–based route or the pack trains and the Mullan Road alternative. The *Montana Post* reported in 1866 that pack-trains over the Mullan Road were "arriving daily."[59] By 1868 and 1869, however, the packing activities began to diminish. St. Louis and Chicago merchants constructed fleets of light draft steamers for use on the upper Missouri River.

The combination of lower freighting rates on the Missouri River and the gradual disrepair of the Mullan Road forced the eventual decline of mule trains along the Mullan route. The government made several attempts over the years to get the road repaired, but by 1868 the road was little more than a trail and according to the *Montana Post,* "in horrible condition at that."[60] As a result the West (Portland and Walla Walla merchants) slowly lost their share of the Montana trade.

Competition between the St. Louis merchants and those from Salt Lake City, however, endured. From 1860 to 1865 the Salt Lake City suppliers enjoyed several advantages, but once upper river steamboating became more dependable, St. Louis businesses began to profit as well. Ultimately there was room for profits from both routes. The Missouri River freighters

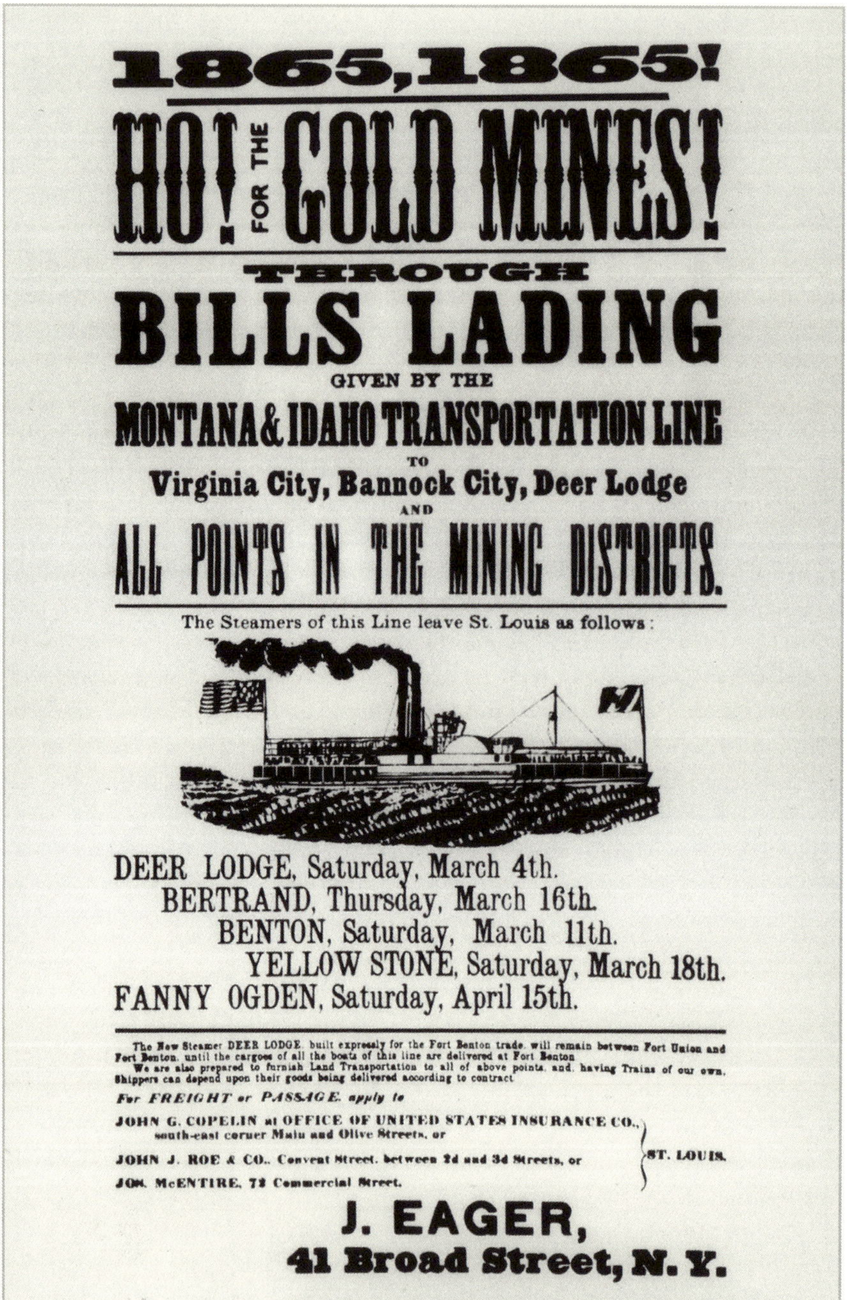

Figure 2.4. Advertisement for the Montana & Idaho Transportation Company. Courtesy of the U.S. Fish and Wildlife Service, DeSoto National Wildlife Refuge, Steamboat Bertrand Collection.

typically transported eastern manufactured goods while the Utah based freighters shipped locally produced grains and produce. As long as the river cooperated and water levels stayed high, river transportation remained more cost effective. Wagon freight was typically 25 cents a pound in the 1860s compared with about 12 cents for steamboat shipments.[61]

Booms are defined by a beginning and an end, or as a bell-shaped curve. Like most booming enterprises, the good times were destined to end in Fort Benton. When upper river steamboating subsided at the end of the 1860s, the reasons were clear. Despite the overall financial success of steamboating, the short freighting season, long, slow journeys, periodic low water, and frequent accidents drove up freighting costs and escalated insurance rates. With operating costs at a premium, there was little margin for error or accidents. In addition, as the 1860s came to a close, the gold rush lost momentum. No longer inundated with food and supply-hungry miners, many trade opportunities vanished along with the miners. Those who remained in Montana tended to take care of their own supply and food needs and were therefore much less dependent on the outside for such commodities. Additionally, 1869 was a hard year for upper Missouri River enterprises in general. A disastrously low water level all but brought river transportation to a halt and the completion of the first transcontinental railroad changed transportation in the United States as a whole forever.[62]

Historian Paul Sharp argued that the collapse reached its lowest point in 1871 when "only six steamboats reached the head of navigation. Declining activity in the gold fields, the completion of the Union Pacific railway, and a disastrously low water level in 1869, paralyzed traffic."[63] By 1873, Fort Benton and the high plains of the upper Missouri were entrenched in a great economic depression, and steamboating on the Missouri seemed a thing of the past.

By 1875, however, Fort Benton was again a busy place with steamboats at the landing and freight wagons waiting to carry cargoes overland toward new markets for freight companies such as I. G. Baker & Company and its rival, T. C. Power & Brother. Just as the drive for the "soft gold" of the fur trade era and the rush to the gold mines drove Fort Benton's economic success during the 1860s, the little river town managed to rebuild itself yet again after the depression of 1873. This time, renewed success married the expansion of the military on both sides of the international boundary to regional freight commerce. Although not as profitable as the gold rush days and certainly not as romantic as the fur trade era, Fort Benton found there was money to be made again.

Instead of fur barons or miners of boom times, the freighter merchants now stood to make great profits. The mercantile commodores made their fortunes by controlling the transportation routes and the means by which goods traveled. Their ability to acquire and hold exclusive government contracts also guaranteed profits. Merchants like the Bakers, Powers, Coulsons, and Pecks built transportation systems and empires that tied together divergent transport technology such as steamers with eastern railroads and bull-trains. The new era on the upper Missouri, the steamboat and stagecoach era of the 1870s, ultimately meant fortunes for those who could both control the transportation networks of the Missouri River west and undercut independent operators from the lucrative government contracts.[64]

Fort Benton's revival in the 1870s, and its economic success through the mid-1880s, was based on the symbiotic relationship between substantial, exclusive American and Canadian government contracts, with the provision of stable and cheap transportation that flowed from the Missouri River.

3

Fort Benton on the Eve of Economic Upturn: Renewed Business Opportunities

We rounded the butte and made fast at the Fort Benton levee on May 27th. Freight was unloaded, a new cargo put aboard and a few days later the "Red Cloud" was again headed down stream.

—Lou Stocking Stewart, remembrance, 1937

The history of Fort Benton and the upper Missouri Region is indelibly linked to the history of I. G. Baker & Company's enterprises, both in the formative years of Fort Benton history (1847–65), and in the region's resurgence in the mid-1870s. I. G. Baker & Company chose the steamboat *Red Cloud* as the flagship for its diverse enterprise.

I. G. Baker, Frontier Visionary

One of Fort Benton's most prominent builders was Isaac Gilbert Baker, founder in 1865–66 of the vastly successful mercantile establishment, I. G. Baker & Company. Originally from Ridgefield, Connecticut, Isaac and his brother George journeyed west to Iowa in 1837.[1] Like so many at the time, Isaac Baker saw the growing potential of the upper Missouri River fur trade. In the mid-1840s, Isaac began his involvement in the upper Missouri region when he joined a fur trading partnership with Josiah Smart and Pierre Chouteau Jr. & Company of St. Louis.[2]

Isaac had a knack for business, enough so that he caught the eye of several of the major merchants of St. Louis. In 1864, the American Fur Company persuaded Baker to give up his efforts as an independent trader and freighter in St. Louis and accept the position of manager at their Fort Benton trading post. Once again, Baker found himself acting as an official agent for Pierre Chouteau Jr.[3] Baker arrived at his new post in Fort Benton in the spring of 1864 on the fur company's steamboat, the *Yellow Stone*. He traveled as far as Cow Island (the highest point reachable on the Missouri River during low water and just downriver from Fort Benton) on the steamer and then proceeded the rest of the way by ox train; the same transportation path that much of his freight took in the years that followed.

Figure 3.1. Isaac Gilbert Baker, ca. 1869. Montana Historical Society, Helena (photograph no. 940-671).

When the ox train carrying Baker pulled into the sleepy town of Benton, there was little more than the Chouteau's trading post and a few cabins and huts scattered about.[4] The buildup of the community from the gold rush was still to come. It was Baker's destiny that the future held that he would play a key role in the further development of the once-dormant Fort Benton.

Baker stayed with Chouteau Jr. & Company through most of 1865. Times had changed, however. The fur trade of the 1840s and 1850s was not what it once was; gold now reigned supreme. Pierre Chouteau Jr. & Company was in the process of dissolving its fur trading empire, and in 1865 the company made several offers to sell its Fort Benton holdings to its newly arrived manager. Baker declined the offers, and Chouteau instead sold his Fort Benton interests to the Northwest Fur Company.

Baker had plans of his own. In 1865 and 1866 he established a merchandising and trading business with his brother, George A. Baker of St. Louis, under the name of I. G. Baker & Brother.[5] The new Baker partnership quickly dominated the local trade in and around Fort Benton. It was, however, a brief victory.

Baker's domination was challenged in 1867 with the arrival of Thomas C. Power in Fort Benton. Power came to Fort Benton with a pile of freight to start a mercantile house of his own, T. C. Power and Brother, but there were no buildings available in which to set up shop. Isaac Baker loaned Power a large tent to protect his merchandise until a store could be built, thus beginning one of the most important relationships in either man's future. The Power and Baker firms spent the next three decades both competing with and helping each other in business.[6]

In 1868, Isaac Baker struck another partnership and, like his association with Thomas Power, one that shaped many of Baker's future business enterprises in Fort Benton. In the fall of 1868, two brothers, William and Charles Conrad of Virginia, arrived in Fort Benton seeking a better way of life than that left to them in the war-torn south. The popular local story tells that when the brothers arrived at Fort Benton, they located a wagon train on its way to Helena. They agreed that one would stay in Fort Benton to see what job opportunities might be found while the other traveled to Helena to see if that town offered better possibilities. The brothers had only a silver dollar between them. They decided to flip the coin to see who would go to Helena. Older brother William won the toss. He and the silver dollar boarded the wagon train that afternoon.[7]

Charles quickly discovered that the majority of the activity in Fort Benton centered on the steamboat levee. By 1868, the freight in Fort Benton was plentiful—either piled high in storage or in the process of being loaded on the ox trains. Freighting seemed to be the business of choice. Still dressed in his travel clothes, Charles began carrying freight with the local roustabouts.

Figure 3.2. The Fort Benton levee, ca. 1868. Kansas State Historical Society, Topeka (photograph no. FM9).

Years later Charles related that he was hoping his enterprise and willingness to work would get him noticed. Indeed, he caught the eye of Isaac Baker. Baker reportedly asked Charles for whom did he work; Charles replied that he worked for no one but that he was looking for a job. Charles must have been a striking contrast to the other young men of Fort Benton, most of whom were either miners or general laborers of one sort or another. Presumably, Baker saw a bright and energetic young man in Charles. Baker told Charles his business was expanding and that he was looking for help managing and running various aspects of his enterprise. He directed Charles to the front office of his store.[8]

When William returned from Helena he found that Charles had not only found them both jobs, but they were solidly positioned within a great opportunity. The two were quickly made clerks in Baker's store and the brothers aggressively sought more responsibility. Eventually they garnered partnerships in Baker's business. Isaac Baker planned to return to St. Louis with his pioneering weary wife and to expand the St. Louis aspect of the company.[9]

Late in 1868, with William and Charles fully ensconced in the business, Isaac Baker moved his family back to St. Louis and turned the daily management of the Fort Benton store and the overland freighting business over to his brother, George. George Baker brought his family to Fort Benton and ably picked up where Isaac left off.

Over the years, Isaac made several trips a year to Fort Benton to check on the Benton house. Never a silent partner, Baker's hands were always directly involved in every aspect of his enterprise. In 1874, after six years of managing the Fort Benton house, George Baker sold his shares of the Fort Benton House to William[10] and Charles[11] and moved to St. Louis to join Isaac and concentrate on the I. G. Baker & Brother business. The former clerks were at long last official partners with Isaac at the Benton store. Their younger brother John eventually joined them. Isaac Baker and the Conrad brothers changed the name of the Benton firm to I. G. Baker & Company.[12]

Meanwhile, in St. Louis, Isaac added a general purchasing and contracting office on Olive Street, in 1873, for the merchandising, contracting, and transportation interests of the firm.[13] Baker also managed the marketing of furs and hides shipped from the upper Missouri region to St. Louis, and from 1876 to1882 he ran the Baker Line of steamboats.[14] Baker and his new partners, the Conrads, recognized that after the region recovered from the collapse in 1873, steamboating on the upper Missouri would mean the difference between simple freighting and making a fortune for their company. In 1876, they established their own line of Missouri River steamers, the Baker Line, to provide a pivotal facet of the company's transportation needs.

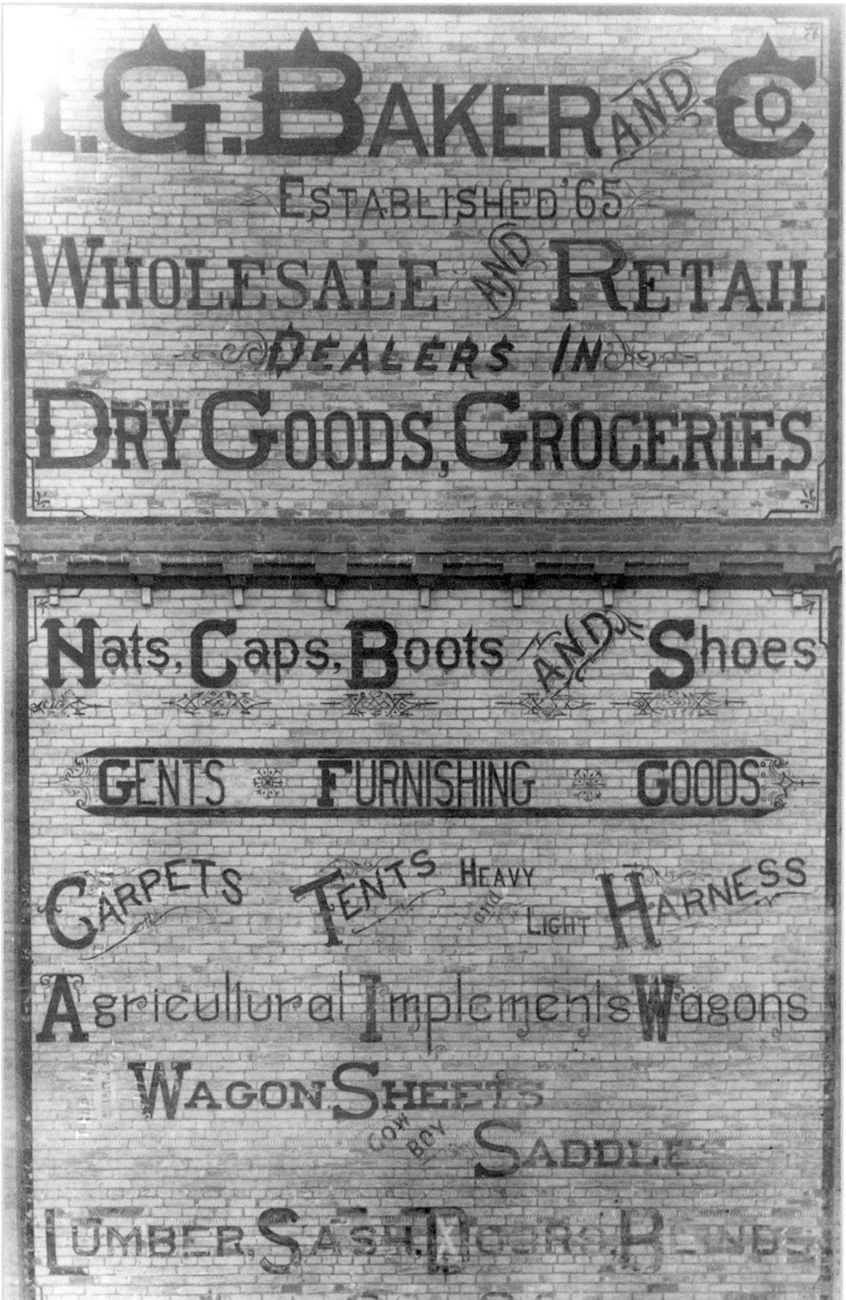

Figure 3.3. I. G. Baker & Company sign painted on the side of a building in Fort Benton, ca. 1884. Montana Historical Society, Helena (photograph no. 947-081).

Shifting Economies on the High Plains

Mining in Montana waned, and the make-up of the river and its associated communities and business ventures changed as well. In 1868, St. Louis lost its hold on the steamboat trade and commerce of the upper Missouri River region. Six weeks before the opening of the navigation season, in March 1868, the Sioux City & Pacific Railroad reached Sioux City. The community of Sioux City quickly claimed itself the new "Gateway to the West," as it also became a hub of commerce from the East Coast via the Great Lakes region with a completed railway from Chicago. St. Louis lost some of its former importance.[15]

Sioux City was linked with Omaha and Chicago, and using Sioux City as the Missouri River's primary port town into the mountains had profound effects on the steamboat business. The Missouri River route to Fort Benton was suddenly 1,000 miles shorter and the journey took twenty fewer days. The obvious advantages of Sioux City soon caught the attention of a number of steamboatmen, including Joab Lawrence, organizer of the Northwest Transportation Company. He moved his enterprise upriver from St. Louis and ran five boats out of Sioux City in 1868. All five boats were a rousing success and all five managed two round trips each to Fort Benton that first season. This was a notable achievement since few St. Louis–based boats could accomplish such a feat within an average navigation season. Freight rates also dropped with the move upriver. Rates once averaging 12 cents a pound from St. Louis were just 5 cents a pound from Sioux City to Fort Benton, and through-rates from Chicago to Fort Benton were only 6 cents a pound.

Lawrence's Sioux City steamboating monopoly was short-lived as other steamboat owners, including William J. Kountz, quickly moved upriver to take advantage of the new railhead. Sioux City's steamboat business was further solidified in 1868 with the government's signing of the Laramie Treaty. The Treaty resulted in the addition of new Indian Agencies and military posts. Both were to be supplied via Missouri River steamboats.[16]

Just as 1868 was a successful year for steamboating, 1869 was a hard year. The river saw its lowest watermark recorded that century. The river was so low that only eighteen of twenty-four steamers made it as far as Fort Benton, and those eighteen boats arrived only because they double-tripped from Dauphin's Rapids. The 200-mile stretch of river below Fort Benton was particularly hazardous—shallow water and extremely rocky even at high water times. To get over some of the rapid areas, including Dauphin's Rapids, steamboats often had to unload portions of their cargo to lighten the load and reduce their draft to get the rest of the way to Fort Benton. They then returned to the drop point to retrieve the remainder of the cargo to be delivered to Fort Benton. The process was commonly referred to as double-tripping, and, although effective, it added time and expense to getting goods upriver. As a result of the extremely low water, that season's freight rates and insurance costs, which had dropped dramatically with the new railhead in Sioux City, suddenly skyrocketed. Adding to this temporary business problem was an even larger, more ominous development. On May 10, 1869, a golden spike was driven at Promontory Summit, Utah. With the completion of the first transcontinental railroad, East finally met West by rail. The United States was suddenly much smaller and Fort Benton's status as an entrepôt of the West was threatened.[17]

As the water level in the Missouri continued to fall through the 1869 season, and freight and insurance rates escalated, Fort Benton seemed doomed to dry up along with the river. The possibility for failure seemed greater with the passing of each season. Only eight boats came to Fort Benton in 1870, eleven in 1871, twelve in 1872, seven in 1873, and only six in 1874. By 1875, even the *Benton Weekly Record* admitted that "the completion of the transcontinental railroad had caused the major portion of the trade to flow northward from Corrine [Utah]."[18]

The fact that goods from the East now traveled cheaply and quickly to Corrine, Utah, by rail and then freighted a short distance to the mines over a well-traveled road, seriously threatened Fort Benton's importance as a freight distribution point.[19] The Union Pacific line ran through southern Wyoming and northern Utah—Montana bound immigrants and freight could now travel by rail to Corinne, 32 miles west of Ogden, at both regular and predictable rates and schedules. From Corinne, immigrants and freight headed north. The route, known as the Corinne–Virginia City Road or the Salt Lake–Montana Trail, connected the Mormon settlements and suppliers to the Montana gold camps.[20]

The establishment of a rail depot at Corrine dramatically transformed the supply business in western Montana. Montana newspapers began boasting of the predictability that the railroad offered. Now, rather than depending on the uncertainty of water levels and steamboat passage, merchants could set their calendars by the arrival of goods. As historians Brigham and Betty Madsen argued, fruit from California and staples from Omaha could be ordered on schedule via the Union Pacific and Central Pacific. From Corinne, a three to four week wagon trip would then deliver the goods to any man's door in Helena. Many in western Montana suddenly felt that civilization was somehow nearer.[21]

Not only were merchants anxious for the possibility of goods arriving on a more predictable schedule, but they also relished the thought of receiving goods well in advance of the opening of the river each spring and later into the fall and early winter. The *Montana Post* noted the Helena merchants' excitement when it printed that "the first receipt of goods by railroad demonstrates the superiority of this means of conveyance over the boats, for light tools and early shipments."[22] In Corinne, the *Utah Reporter* noted that on July 23rd a freight train consisting of twenty teams left for Helena, and the paper predicted that Corinne would become the great transfer point for goods to Montana.[23]

By November of 1869, the Union Pacific was running six to eight freight trains daily through Corinne. As a result, it took no time at all for several big overland freighting outfits to start heading north. Soon, Hugh Kirkendall, the Northwest Transportation Company's "Rocky Mountain Dispatch," the Far West Freight Line, and the giant establishment of the West, the Diamond R, filled the freight trains. As soon as the trains arrived at the railhead, the overland freighters loaded their wagons and turned their teams north to western Montana. As more freight reached Montana from Corinne, the merchants of Helena turned away from goods delivered through Fort Benton. Through the first five years after the completion of the transcontinental railroad, Union Pacific shipments to Montana via Utah remained constant. Between 6 and 7 million pounds of goods were shipped to Montana each year via the railroad. If Missouri River freighting and its associated merchants hoped to compete and climb out of the economic slump of the early 1870s, something drastic had to be done.[24]

In 1875, the Fort Benton trade made a remarkable comeback. Historian Alton Oviatt suggested that the answer lie not in recovering the markets of the southwestern Montana mining region lost to the railroad and the overland route from Corinne, but rather by finding entirely new markets that were still better served by the Missouri River.[25] In the early 1870s, the two rivals T. C. Power & Brother and I. G. Baker & Company, and a few remaining independent operators, found new markets by supplying the Judith Basin, the mines at Maiden and Barker, Lewistown, Sun River, the agencies for the Blackfoot and Assiniboine tribes, the United States Military, and the Canadian Northwest Mounted Police.

When the Canadian government established mounted police at Forts MacLeod, Walsh, Lethbridge, Medicine Hat, and Calgary, I. G. Baker & Company was quick to realize the potential profit for supplying the remote Canadian northwest region via the Whoop-Up Trail from Fort Benton

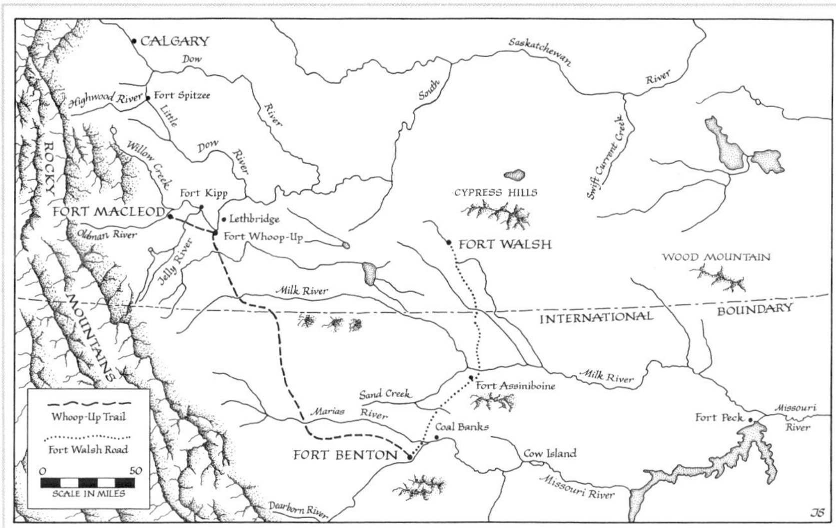

Map 3.1. The Whoop-Up Trail. Drawn by Jack Scott, 1999.

north to Fort MacLeod.[26] Oviatt aptly argued that "not only was the steamboat traffic of the late 1870s and early 1880s in the main with a different region, but the trade itself was different in character."[27]

With new opportunities, the upper Missouri River was once again the most economical and practical way to move goods in the region and would revive Fort Benton's trade.[28] During the boom years from 1875 to 1883, the Whoop-Up Trail carried one-third of the freight handled through Fort Benton; I. G. Baker & Company was one of the most prolific suppliers.

The economic impact of the river commerce on Fort Benton was clear. Paul Sharp summed up the importance of the new markets in the Fort Benton area when he argued that their opening in the mid-1870s profoundly altered life at Fort Benton. No longer was Fort Benton a small-scale supply town, and gone were the gold rush stampedes and the fur trade of old. It was the merchants who now reigned supreme with baron enterprises such as I. G. Baker & Company and T. C. Power and Brother fully in charge of the account books and manifest lists.[29]

The lifeblood of Fort Benton once again flowed via the Missouri River. In importance, the Mullan Road, although still used, was replaced by the Whoop-Up Trail. Instead of going south, goods now headed for the far north of the Canadian plains. The chief controllers of this extensive trade were the Baker and Power firms because their own steamboats carried their supplies. The fortunes of these companies were intertwined with the growth of Fort Benton and the steamboating enterprise on the upper Missouri in the post–Civil War era.[30]

Scarlet Tunics on the Prairie

One of the most important aspects of Fort Benton's economic recovery in the 1870s, as well as the prosperity of I. G. Baker & Company, was the arrival of the Canadian North-West Mounted Police (NWMP) in the Whoop-Up country. The recently formed Canadian Confederation, known as the Dominion of Canada, established the North-West Mounted Police in 1873 to bring law and order to the vast western lands (originally known as Rupert's Land and later as the North-West Territory) acquired in 1869 from the Hudson's Bay Company. At the time of the purchase, the Dominion government knew full well the problems they just acquired—law and order on the frontier was a major concern on both sides of the border and had been since the Territory was first organized.

In 1670, King Charles II of England granted a charter to the Hudson's Bay Company to trade and settle the area of Canada draining into Hudson Bay. The charter granted the Company almost sovereign powers over an expanse of land the actual size and area of which would not be known for almost another century. American fur traders, excluded from the company's domain, later referred to the initials of the Company, HBC, as "Here Before Christ." By 1821, HBC had smothered the competition and was ruling the vast territory both economically and politically. By mid-century, however, incursion into the trading territory by settlers from both sides of the international boundary became a problem. In 1869, the difficulty of opening land for settlement became such an issue within Canada that the Company transferred a large section of its territorial holdings to the Dominion government for the sum of £300,000.[31]

When the Dominion government purchased the Hudson Bay lands in 1869, they were well aware that the governmental infrastructure, men, or police necessary to govern the new territory were nonexistent. In addition to peaceful settlers moving into the area, reckless and lawless groups of traders from the United States were crossing the border to get rich from a still-flourishing Canadian fur trade or by selling liquor to the Canadian Indians.[32] This continued the difficulties in Anglo/American relations brought on by the American Civil War and the ill fated Fenian invasion of Lower Canada in June 1866. The Fenian's were a group of Irish Americans who invaded Canada as an act against the British government.[33]

Matters came to a head in May 1873, when a battle between a party of white hunters (wolfers) and traders from Fort Benton and a band of northern Assiniboine Indians took place in the low-lying hills of southern Saskatchewan. The incident, commonly referred to as the Cypress Hills Massacre, touched off an international incident.[34]

Most scholars of western Canadian history agree that the Cypress Hills Massacre forced Sir John MacDonald, Prime Minister of Canada, to implement a previously designed but nonimplemented 1871 plan calling for a mounted police force.[35] Historian R. Charles Macleod has advanced a different view that deserves attention. He suggested that the formation of the NWMP had roots that ran far deeper than the Cypress Hills incident.

Macleod argued that the formation of the NWMP was just one of many pieces of Sir John A. Macdonald's development strategy, his *National Policy,* the key to which was the peaceful development of western Canada. Without a peaceful environment, Macdonald argued, the railroads would not be built into the western interior, eastern capitalists could not be induced to invest, nor would homesteaders be persuaded to settle and develop the Canadian frontier. This frontier was notoriously plagued with crime, disorder, and the constant fear of Indian attack. The Americans had already demonstrated that settlement and development could take place despite these conditions, but the American method was costly. The price of controlling just the Indian element was costing the government 20 million dollars a year by 1870. The Dominion could not afford such risk; with a total yearly budget of just over 19 million dollars, an Indian war of any size would have devastated the Dominion government.[36]

Most Canadian officials recognized these problems. The question, therefore, became what to do about them. The very survival of an infant Canada was tied to successfully opening its vast western territories. Canada's nearest neighbor, the United States, had failed to occupy their western territories despite seemingly limitless resources. How could cash-poor Canada hope to accomplish such a feat as the peaceful occupation of the western plains? Sir John Macdonald thought he knew the answer.[37]

Macdonald argued for the creation of a force: approximately three hundred men who would be trained as both soldiers and police, much like the Royal Forces of Ireland and India. Macdonald's force would be armed and trained as cavalry and could fight if need be. Their main focus, however, would be as policemen, to prevent crime from developing to the point where a trained army would need to intervene. The police would be centrally controlled, yet they would act as magistrates and pass judgment on criminals, as well as apprehending them.[38]

The task at hand for such a force was great indeed, but one that would be crucial if the Dominion hoped to hang onto western Canada. By the time the government made the HBC purchase, the threat of losing its newly acquired territory was quite real. The commerce of Canada's southwestern prairies already belonged to Montana, and there was a growing concern that the Red River area was becoming an annex of Minnesota.[39]

The only hope of discouraging a gradual American invasion was to establish a solid Canadian military presence throughout western Canada. Macdonald's growing concerns were fully realized within months of the Dominion takeover of portions of the Northwest Territory. As feared, the Red River area proved volatile. Conflicts erupted over voting and the formation of government in the newly organized province of Manitoba between the native French-speaking, Roman Catholic métis and the growing number of English-speaking Protestant settlers moving in from eastern Ontario. The conflict grew so out of control that, in the spring of 1870, the Dominion government was forced to send troops to the new province in an effort to keep the peace.

The Manitoba issues became a glaring example of the possible problems associated with first contacts between white settlers and indigenous peoples, even those so settled as the métis. Macdonald was quick to point out that "with emigrants of all nations flowing into that country, we are in constant danger of an Indian war, and that commenced God knows where it may end. This may be prevented by the early organization of a Mounted Police."[40]

Despite the military presence, the political climate of Manitoba remained delicate. In 1871, the citizens of Manitoba found themselves preparing to fend off a possible Fenian invasion, and, much to the surprise and presumably the shame of most Manitobans, the majority of those who volunteered to fight with the military were the métis. Although the Fenian threat passed, the incident served only to focus anti-French resentment. This resentment finally came to a head in the election of 1872, which was marked by pitched street battles and extensive property damage despite the presence of the militia. Clearly something had to be done. Macdonald argued that the Manitoba turmoil was just the type of situation that a police force could have prevented. Alexander Morris, the first chief justice of Manitoba and later its lieutenant governor, agreed. Morris began to harass Macdonald, asking that the Militia be retained in Manitoba and a police force of at least one hundred red-coated men be established as well.[41] In addition to Morris's support, Macdonald's plan gained weight from two other developments.

The stakes were raised in the development of the Canadian West in 1872, when the first Pacific Railway Company was formed. A peaceful building climate would be necessary if any hope of success existed for the venture. Next, Canada's top military man, the adjutant general of the Canadian Militia, Colonel Patrick Robertson-Ross, returned from an extensive survey of the Canadian northwest.[42] The Colonel's report supported both Morris and Macdonald's estimates of the western situation.[43] The Colonel recommended a regiment of 550 mounted men to be divided between several locations. The largest contingent of this regiment would be stationed in what is now southern Alberta, along the international boundary, to try and deal with the growing issue of American whiskey traders.[44]

Historian R. Charles Macleod argued, therefore, that at most, the Cypress Hills Massacre had only a minor influence in the Dominion decision to deploy the mounted police force. Following the 1872 Robertson-Ross report and with the continued pleas from Morris, Parliament finally debated the establishment of Macdonald's Mounted Police force in the spring of 1873. In April, Parliament passed the Police Act without a dissenting vote. Only in July did Canadian officials learn about the Cypress Hills Massacre. Macleod suggested that the primary reason for the deployment of the police to western Canada was linked to a growing concern that hostilities would take place not from the Indians but between the often-fanatical English settlers and the very excitable Indian-French settlers in the Canadian West. There was also the concern that the American military would cross the border in its attempt to gain control of the American based liquor trade.[45]

Historian Paul Sharp accurately portrayed the magnitude of the job ahead of the NWMP when he suggested that eliminating the notorious whiskey traffic was only one of the force's immediate concerns. Beyond the responsibilities of patrolling boundaries, collecting customs, and halting smuggling, the police had the enormous task of gaining the respect and confidence of Canada's native Indian tribes. A primary goal of the NWMP was to ease the natives' transition from a nomadic way of life to a sedentary reservation existence. All of this was to be accomplished without the bloodshed and tragedy so prevalent south of the border. These objectives had the clear purpose of opening the country so that the steel of the Canadian Pacific Railway could be laid and the area developed for permanent white settlement.[46]

I. G. Baker & Company and the NWMP

The newly trained NWMP arrived in the Whoop-Up country only after many delays. Spending the winter of 1873–74 at Fort Dufferin, Manitoba, a force consisting of twenty-four officers, led by Lieutenant Colonel George

Figure 3.4. Colonel Macleod of the Canadian North-West Mounted Police. National Archives of Canada, Ottawa (photograph no. PA2015696).

Arthur French and Major James Macleod, with 295 police started west from Manitoba on July 8, 1874. Their journey, known as the Long March, was a near disaster.[47] By September the contingent of Mounted Police had become lost and were on the verge of starvation on the Canadian frontier. The troops did not know that they were only a few miles from the well-traveled Whoop-Up Trail and only 75 miles from the whiskey post, Fort Whoop-Up, when snow began to fall on September 9th. The contingent turned south to Three Buttes, or Sweet Grass Hills, a few miles north of the Canadian border. A group of seven men, including French and Macleod, headed south in search of Fort Benton to get help. The party arrived at Fort Benton on September 24th, and it was then that many scholars suggest the long and profitable association between the Mounties and I. G. Baker & Company began.[48] Long-time Fort Benton historian Joel Overholser, however, argued that the NWMP's immediate association with I. G. Baker & Company was by no means accidental, as most believed.[49]

I. G. Baker & Company contacted the Dominion government concerning the NWMP prior to the force's arrival on the Canadian plains in September 1874. In a 1916 reminiscence, Shirley Ashby, a former I. G. Baker & Company clerk, recalled that, prior to sending troops west, the Canadian government recognized and tried to deal with an obvious supply problem. There were no supply or trading houses in the Belly River country (the area of the Canadian western plains just north of Montana Territory), and supplies had to be secured via the Missouri River. Ashby understood that the Canadian government had searched for a reputable American firm that would supply the needs of the police. The Dominion was directed to New York to communicate with Robert W. Donnell who, a few years earlier, had run a large wholesale business on Bridge Street in Helena, Montana Territory. Donnell recommended I. G. Baker & Company, saying, "there was not a finer man in the United States than I. G. Baker. . . . they would find him very trustworthy[,] reliable[,] and [an] honest man in every respect. . . . They could be supplied with anything that they wanted from a Jews harp to a threshing machine."[50]

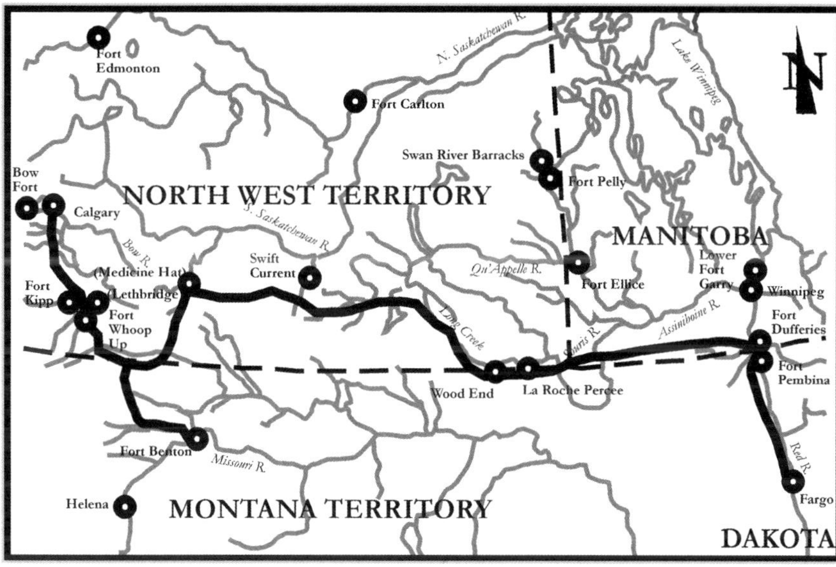

Map 3.2. The Long March west in 1874. Drawn by Nathan Richards, 2004.

In May 1873, more than a year before the police began their Long March, the Royal Canadian government followed Donnell's advice by writing to I. G. Baker & Company requesting quotations of freight rates.[51] The Baker firm responded to the Dominion's request, and, as events played out, a connection of great consequences began. Ashby finished by noting that when the Canadian North-West Mounted Police linked up with the Baker firm that "the big trade began and a fortune was founded."[52]

In addition to Donnell's good will, I. G. Baker & Company had another advantage, a friend within the Canadian government. Lieutenant Governor Edgar Dewdney used his influence to secure Canadian contracts and favors for the Baker firm. Dewdney was the first lieutenant governor of the North-West Territories and, as such, had knowledge of the firms across the border.[53] In return for helping I. G. Baker & Company secure Canadian contracts, Dewdney was often rewarded with shares in various Baker & Company business ventures. As Sharp so aptly put it, "In return, he earned handsome investments in Benton enterprise. On one occasion, the Canadian official received fifty shares in the Benton National Bank 'to get a deposit by it of $100,000 or $200,000 from the Canadian government.'"[54] Connections with the Canadian government proved useful for years to come.

By the time the starved and tired Mounties arrived at Fort Benton in September 1874, I. G. Baker & Company was more than prepared to provide them with a hearty welcome. Over dinner, the Conrad brothers, William and Charles, listened to Colonel French and Major Macleod describe the plight of the rest of their men. Charles Conrad agreed that I. G. Baker & Company would furnish all the emergency supplies French's force needed on credit and would accept payment on such terms as French could later arrange with the Canadian government. Wagons were quickly loaded with supplies for the Mounties and their horses. With Charles heading up the resupply party, the wagons returned with French, Macleod, and their men to Three Buttes.[55]

The arrival of the NWMP in western Canada had an immediate impact on two groups: the whiskey traders and the Canadian Indians. From Isaac Baker, French and Macleod learned that the impending arrival of the Mounties in the west had already paralyzed the whiskey trade and that it was likely that the Mounties would encounter little resistance from the notorious traders. Baker reported that, "The effect of the Expedition was sudden and decisive, on Col. French's arrival at Benton, one of the Traders sent a message to his partner to remove all whiskey out of the way."[56]

Additionally, upon arrival at Three Buttes, Charles Conrad found not only hungry Mounties and horses but also Blackfeet Indians surrounding the entire Mounties camp. The Indians were curious about the red-coated newcomers they had been hearing so much about. Hoping to ease Indian resistance to the Mounties, the Dominion government sent Reverend John McDougal ahead to inform the Blackfeet that the Queen's Police would soon arrive. McDougal told the Blackfeet that the Mounties were sent to protect the Indians from the hostile American traders and that the Police did not necessarily expect the Blackfeet to become military allies but only to be friendly.[57] Charles Conrad and Jerry Potts, the half-Blackfoot guide the NWMP picked up in Fort Benton, introduced the Mounties to the Blackfeet and a long Indian-Police relationship began.

After feeding both the hungry Mounties and their horses, Charles Conrad and the NWMP contingent finally made it to the whiskey post, Fort Whoop-Up, on October 9. Just as Isaac Baker predicted, word had preceded the Police force's arrival at Fort Whoop-Up, and rather than the five hundred desperados, wolfers, and illegal whiskey traders who typically occupied the post, the party found an almost-deserted fort.[58]

The same day the Mounties and Conrad reached Fort Whoop-Up, the *Herald* announced that I. G. Baker & Company had won the contract to supply the Canadian Mounted Police for the year. Much to its dismay, the long-established Hudson's Bay Company found it was surrendering the southwestern Canadian prairies to I. G. Baker & Company and their

Figure 3.5. Fort Macleod, ca. 1874. National Archives of Canada, Ottawa (photograph no. 01762).

better-established transportation networks.[59] To fill the first contracted order, Isaac Baker purchased groceries, hardware, clothing, and miscellaneous goods totaling £40,000 for immediate shipment across the border.[60]

The nexus between I. G. Baker & Company and the NWMP became quite clear when Conrad and the Mounties arrived at Fort Whoop-Up.[61] Upon arrival in October 1874, Colonel French offered to buy Fort Whoop-Up to serve as Police headquarters. When Fort Whoop-Up's owner John Healy's asking price of $25,000 proved too high, Conrad suggested that, rather than negotiating, I. G. Baker & Company should just build a new post, Fort Macleod, on the Oldman River, for the Police. Before Fort Macleod was even completed, I. G. Baker & Company built a store near the post.

Ultimately, the Baker firm followed the NWMP across the Canadian plains, building police posts and stores at Calgary,[62] Fort Walsh, Lethbridge, Medicine Hat, and Cypress Creek. On April 22, 1875, Assistant Surgeon R. B. Nevitt, stationed at Fort Macleod, noted in letters to his fiancée, Elizabeth Eleanor Beaty,[63] that,

> Yesterday Conrad's [I. G. Baker & Company] train came in, leaving Benton on the 26th of March. They have just managed to get in. Conrad had traded out everything; his store was as bare as the place could be. The wagons had hardly come into the corral before crowds of Indians came down with four or five pack horses apiece packed with robes to

trade. In a very short while the goods were displayed on the shelves and a brisk trade began and has kept up all day.[64]

The Hudson's Bay Company also noted both the success and the impact that I. G. Baker & Company had in the Canadian West. Just as at Fort Macleod, the Baker enterprise at Fort Calgary did well. An HBC official noted that "we have several small buildings about a quarter the size of Baker's. Baker has a large supply of goods on hand, their present stock being about $25,000. We had to buy what we wanted there, owing to there being nothing in the H. B. store."[65]

The Baker firm eventually served as supplier, paymaster, builder, banker, and postman for the Canadian North-West Mounted Police. During the 1874–75 season the Canadian government spent more than $333,000 for supplies, horses, and building materials from Baker & Company.[66] In addition to supplying the police posts, Baker & Company also shipped 15,000 buffalo robes traded at Fort Macleod during the winter of 1874–75 to Fort Benton.[67] The Baker firm retained this exclusive contract with the NWMP even after the arrival of the Canadian Pacific Railroad in Calgary in 1883.[68]

The Fort Benton Transportation Company—Launching the *Benton*

For anyone still unsure of the sustaining impact of the Canadian markets on Montana's economic recovery, there can be little doubt regarding the next phase of Benton's renewal. In November 1874, local papers announced that "T. C. Power & Co., I. G. Baker & Co., and other capitalists have ordered a light draft steamboat, first class in all appointments for the Upper Missouri River, and that the boat is to be ready for the spring trade of 1875."[69] This notice highlighted the first steamboat to be owned by a Montana company. This ownership heralded a significant departure from traditional river transportation patterns of the previous steamboat era on the Missouri.

The boat that the newspaper alluded to turned out to be the steamer *Benton*.[70] The stern-wheeler was the first of eight vessels to carry the new Benton Packet Line's "Block P" insignia (T. C. Power & Brother's Fort Benton Transportation Company). A new era in upper river steamboating began as Block P boats, and shortly thereafter I. G. Baker & Company (Baker Line) boats, took control of the upper river shipping. For decades downriver companies such as Durfee and Peck, Kountz, and the Coulson Lines held sway over the Missouri.[71] During the 1875 freighting season, I. G. Baker & Company experimented with both running and administrating several

Figure 3.6. Advertisement announcing the departure of the steamboat *Benton* in 1877. *Bismarck Semi-Weekly Tribune,* April 11, 1877.

steamers. The Power and Baker–owned *Benton* proved a huge success; as the season progressed the I. G. Baker & Company office in St. Louis signaled the addition of more company-operated steamboats when they began advertising as agents for the steamers *C. W. Mead* and the *Fontenelle.*[72]

In 1875, the *St. Louis Democrat* reported that the amount of freight purchased heading for Fort Benton had increased dramatically—a large increase: in fact, as much as the previous three years combined. The paper concluded that the upper Missouri trade must be returning to its original channels (like the boom years of the 1860s).[73] That year I. G. Baker & Company shipped a large amount of furs[74] out of the territory on a variety of steamers including the *Benton,* and for the first time company vessels transported officers and recruits for the NWMP via the Missouri River to Fort Benton.[75]

The *Benton Weekly Record* reported that I. G. Baker & Company's freight shipment for Fort Macleod in the last week of July 1875 reached 65,000 pounds. The freighting needs of the firm were so great in1875 that, in addition to the three boats already under contract, Baker contracted the *Josephine,*[76] from a competing line, to carry the overflow freight.[77]

Just as 1875 signaled renewed growth in Fort Benton shipping, 1876 proved to be a boom year. In addition to the supplies for the NWMP, I. G. Baker & Company vessels brought cargoes up the Missouri River that were never before seen. Manifests included rich parlor suits, elegant chamber sets, and an almost unlimited variety of articles for the kitchen.[78] A notice in the *Benton Weekly Record,* perhaps planted by an I. G. Baker & Company agent, noted the company's freighting accomplishments. The stock, he wrote,

> consists of a large assortment of Centennial clocks; Star Spangled banner and other patterns of dress goods of new and elegant designs; clothing of stylish cut' hats and Caps; boots and shoes; carpets; hardware; and in fact anything and everything that our citizens are likely to need. We venture to say that the stock of furniture now in the warehouses of this firm surpasses anything of the kind ever brought to the Territory. Bedroom suits, dressing case sets, marble top bureaus and wash stands, office chairs, rockers, stoves, cooking utensils, and in fact an endless variety of everything that a man, woman or child can want.[79]

In addition to the wide variety of local freight, I. G. Baker & Company continued to expand its Canadian involvement in1876 by becoming paymaster for the Police divisions. Once again, the Fort Benton firm monopolized on the Hudson's Bay Company's apparent failure to fulfill the first contract issued for the NWMP payroll at forts Macleod and Calgary. In June of 1876, Isaac Baker acknowledged an agreement recently made with Assistant Commissioner Irvine to meet the failed payments of the Hudson's Bay Company and to issue pay for the force for the remainder of the year.[80]

By contract with the Dominion government, I. G. Baker & Company agreed to furnish the police payroll for Cypress Hills, Fort Macleod, and Fort Calgary. Baker & Company delivered the funds to the commanding officer of each post, who then provided the firm with receipts of the funds in triplicate, one copy to be forwarded to the Canadian Secretary of State. The payroll venture proved extremely profitable for I. G. Baker & Company. Upon receipt of Baker's payroll vouchers, the amount paid out plus a commission of 2 percent was applied to Baker & Company's account at the Bank of Montreal. The average pay expenditure for four divisions of NWMP was approximately $5,700 per month, which yielded an estimated $1,400 for the Baker firm in commissions per year.[81] By the end of the 1876 freighting season, I. G. Baker & Company had realized a solid new source of income and laid the foundation for a transportation empire that commanded the Missouri River by steamboats and the Canadian plains by wagon train.

4

A New Whistle on the Wind: The *Red Cloud* on the Missouri, 1877

The "Red Cloud," of the Baker Line, was one of the largest boats on the river and one of the most palatial.

—Lou Stocking Stewart, remembrance, 1937

I. G. Baker & Company learned many lessons from their successes with the 1875–76 season. First and foremost, the Fort Benton firm recognized the key to sustained growth in the post–gold rush era was tied to dominating local trade. In addition to revitalizing a solid footing in upper river steamboating, by 1875 Fort Benton was the starting point for a dozen well-established trails radiating from Fort Benton like the spokes of a giant wheel. As with river transportation, overland freighting was big business—few independents could adequately compete against the overland giants of I. G. Baker & Company; T. C. Power & Brother; Murphy, Neel and Company; and the ever-daunting Diamond R. Every spring, each of these enterprises dispatched hundreds of wagons, and with them, the thousands of oxen and mules that kept the freight moving out of Fort Benton.[1]

The Baker & Company wagon and bull trains ran along the Whoop-Up Trail as often as there was freight and the weather permitted. On January 5, 1877, the *Benton Weekly Record* reported that Baker trains were pulling out for Fort Macleod with 3,000 pounds of supplies before the next big snow set in.[2] I. G. Baker & Company's Canadian business was so large and crucial to the firm's success that Charles Conrad took up long-term residence at Fort Macleod.[3] In February the firm was busy rounding up beef cattle for shipment north along the same trail that their freight often went.[4] More goods followed that winter and spring. In March, Baker & Company sent 10,000 pounds of merchandise, including a large assortment of agricultural implements, to Fort Macleod. Another 5,000 pounds of goods followed two weeks later.[5] All this freight was sent up the Whoop-Up Trail before the first steamboat even arrived at the levee for the season.

Building on its steamboating and freighting experience during the 1875 and 1876 seasons, I. G. Baker & Company took additional steps to round out its freighting enterprise. In early 1876, the company won permission from the U.S. government to establish a bonded line for the shipment of goods to the Northwest Territories. T. C. Power actually established the first bonded line in Montana in 1875 as a way to avoid international trade tariffs. He also hoped that his scheme would push out his competitors for the Canadian markets, especially I. G. Baker & Company.

Power secured a permit to ship goods from eastern Canada or England through the United States to western Canadian customers under a $100,000 bond deposited in Washington, D.C. Power recognized that lowering the tariffs paid by American firms shipping Canadian goods back to Canada via the Missouri River would be essential in pushing out the Hudson's Bay Company and other would-be Winnipeg competitors. By the same token, his scheme would only work if he could secure an exclusive permit for this trade. Try as he might, he knew that his major rival I. G. Baker & Company was also attempting to secure the same deal in Washington. Power stated, "I understand that I. G. B[aker] is after the same favor."[6] As later events proved, Power's political maneuvering did not secure him the monopoly he wanted. Several other Fort Benton firms managed to secure the same privileges, and I. G. Baker & Company established its bonded line in 1876.

The Baker Bonded Line ran by rail from Chicago, Duluth, and St. Louis to Bismarck and Benton via the Missouri River and then on to the Canadian forts of Macleod and Walsh.[7] After obtaining the rights to open trade within the Canadian markets, I. G. Baker & Company sold part of its interests in the *Benton* and Power's Benton Packet Line in early 1877 (George A. Baker, Isaac's brother, remained a partner and served as secretary of the Block P line for many years).[8] I. G. Baker & Company leased the *Fannie Tatum* and in April that same year the company bought the steamboat *Red Cloud* for $25,000, thus inaugurating the Baker Line of steamboats.[9]

The steamboat *Red Cloud* was built in 1873 for the Evansville & Tennessee River Packet Company by the famed Howard boatyard in Jeffersonville, Indiana.[10] The steamer was a stern-wheel, wooden-hull packet (combina-

Figure 4.1. The steamboat *Red Cloud* on the Missouri River, ca. 1877. Murphy Library, University of Wisconsin–La Crosse (photograph no. 4559).

tion passenger and freight hauler), originally 178 feet long by 34.5 feet wide with a 5.2-foot mean depth of hold. She was rated at 324 tons (cubic capacity of the hull and above deck space). The boat had two engines 16.5 inches in diameter with a 5.5-foot stroke. In addition to the main deck and boiler deck, the boat had a significant texas deck (the deck above the boiler deck; the texas deck was typically used as officer quarters and was often missing on Mountain steamboats) and luxurious passenger accommodations. Construction of the steamer cost the Evansville & Tennessee River Packet Company $26,375.00.[11]

The *Evansville Journal* advertised that the *Red Cloud* had elegant cabin and stateroom appointments and that her officers ranked among the best boatmen of the age. The steamer was launched from the port of Evansville on December 27, 1873, to become one of three boats owned by the company. The *Red Cloud* began running Evansville to Florence, Alabama, and back once a week.[12] In 1877, the steamer was sold to I. G. Baker & Company of Fort Benton, Montana Territory, where it was to play a vital role in the resurgence of the upper Missouri Mountain trade.[13]

I. G. Baker & Company owned a seven-sixteenths share in the boat, John W. Conrad of Fort Benton owned a seven-sixteenths share, and George A. Baker of St. Louis owned a one-eighth share.[14] It was common for ownership of steamboats to be divided into shares or "steamboat stock," as historian Louis Hunter called it. Divided ownership helped distribute the burden of costs (maintenance, insurance, personnel, and such) and allowed for ownership to change hands more easily. However, ownership was often spread across vast geographical distances, making it more difficult to locate all owners in settling claims. Hunter also suggested that dividing ownership often formed business ties between large commercial centers such as St. Louis or New Orleans and the smaller river communities where shareholders often resided.[15]

The arrival of the *Red Cloud* was a much-anticipated event on the upper Missouri. The *Benton Weekly Record* began the hype when it began running the first advertisements for the boat in April. On May 5, 1877, the paper reported that the previous year the steamer was "considered the crack boat of the Tennessee River—Her passenger accommodations are said to be superior to those of any other boat on the upper Missouri."[16] The *Bismarck Semi-Weekly Tribune* carefully watched the boat's progress up the river. On May 9, the paper reported that the *Red Cloud* had left Sioux City for Bismarck on May 1 and was expected soon.[17] The journey took longer than anticipated and the Bismarck paper noted that the steamer was overdue.[18] The boat finally arrived at the Bismarck levee on June 8, 1877; the paper reported that the boat was well adapted for upper Missouri River traffic and that she should do well on her first Missouri River journey.[19] By June 15, the *Red Cloud* was reported about 15 miles below Buford and on June 18, the boat was passed below Poplar Creek by the steamer *Key West*.[20]

On June 22, 1877, the steamboat finally made its first appearance at the Fort Benton levee, with famed steamboatman, William Massie, serving as pilot.[21] The *Benton Weekly Record* hailed the boat a success for bringing in 320 tons of freight and 22 passengers to Fort Benton.[22] The Fort Benton *Record* reported that the citizens of Fort Benton expected the *Red Cloud* to be an unusually fine craft, "but we venture to say few of the residents of our little burg were prepared to believe that Messrs. Baker & Co.'s steamer was anything like the elegant floating palace that came to our wharf at 7:30 this morning."[23] When the vessel headed back downriver to Bismarck, she carried another 240 tons of freight consigned to the Northern Pacific Railroad,

Table 4.1. Manifest of the steamboat *Red Cloud*
June 22, 1877, Bismarck to Fort Benton

T. C. Power & Co.	1 box merchandise
M. Renig	4 bbl syrup
W. F. Chadwick	1 cask wine
Kinna & Jack	1 box hardware
S. H. Osborn	144 packages drugs
S. C. Ashby	1 buggy
A. M. Holter & Bro.	37 packages iron steel
Dr. R. A. Wells	18 packages H. H. goods
I. G. Baker & Co., Fort Benton	4,725 packages
I. G. Baker & Co., Fort McLeod, Canada	352 packages
I. G. Baker & Co., Fort Walsh, Canada	10 packages

Benton Weekly Record, June 22, 1877

Table 4.2. Manifest of the steamboat *Red Cloud*
June 28, 1877, Fort Benton to Bismarck

Mr. T. M. Barret, Sedalia, Mo.	1 box merchandise
Mrs. Boyd, Liverpool, England	1 bale furs
N. B. Perkins, Bryon, Ohio	1 bale furs
H. Richison, Ottawa, Canada	1 bale bear skins
Pope, Cole & Co., Baltimore, Md.	161 bags ore
C. Stinson and Frechette, Montreal, Canada	1 bale bear skins, 1 chest furs
Harding, Grey & Dewey, Boston, Mass.	34 bales wool
M. S. Books & Co., St. Louis, Mo.	702 dry hides
I. G. Baker & Co., St. Louis, Mo.	2,166 bales buffalo robes and skins
George A. Baker, St. Louis, Mo.	90 bales buffalo robes and skins
Claxton & Co., Montreal, Canada	480 buffalo robes

Bismarck Semi-Weekly Tribune, June 29, 1877

along with soldiers bound for Dauphin's Rapids and forty-six passengers reportedly anxious to ride the new boat.[24]

The initial success of the *Red Cloud* was an indication of the firm's business acumen. Part of I. G. Baker & Company's success as merchandisers and freighters was due to the ferocious way they pursued contracts. In 1877, for example, I. G. Baker & Company of Fort Benton engaged in a bidding war with I. G. Baker & Company of St. Louis to secure a freighting contract with Davis & Wallace, a Helena grocery firm. In 1876, I. G. Baker & Company did all of the supplying and freighting for the Helena grocer and wished to continue that service in 1877. To offset the possibility that Davis

& Wallace would find better prices in shipping direct from St. Louis, rather than buying after goods arrived at the Baker firm's Fort Benton store (which would have external freight costs added to the Benton wholesale price), I. G. Baker & Company set up negotiations for Davis & Wallace with George A. Baker's Commission and Brokerage service in St. Louis.

The irony of this arrangement is that not only was George Baker a brother and former partner with Isaac in Fort Benton, but in 1877, he was a partner in Isaac's I. G. Baker & Company St. Louis house. He also served as secretary for Power's Block P and ran his brokerage firm out of Isaac's St. Louis building at 219 Olive Street. George Baker thus funneled any business he secured back through I. G. Baker & Company houses in both St. Louis and Fort Benton. Ultimately, I. G. Baker & Company found it more profitable to supply Davis & Wallace directly through the Fort Benton house by agreeing to charge the Helena grocer the same rate on freight as I. G. Baker & Company paid for its own freight.[25] A fine example of frontier business at its best.

High Times in Fort Benton

By the time July 1877 rolled around, it was more than clear to most citizens in Fort Benton that 1877 was going to be a boom year, reminiscent of times past. The steamers owned or leased by the Baker and Power firms were advertised with the lowest rates on the river; $15 deck passage and $35 for cabin passage. The *Benton Weekly Record* reported that the officers of the *Benton, Red Cloud,* and *Fannie Tatum* would "spare neither trouble nor expense to insure the comfort of their passengers."[26] Not only was steamboat freight rapidly piling up at the levee, but also the town itself seemed ready to burst at its seams.

Fort Benton finally got its first building not constructed of adobe, logs, or wood, when the Helena firm Kleinschmidt & Bros. established a branch store at Fort Benton. The company built a 35 foot x 140 foot concrete warehouse, the largest in the Territory, from which to ship approximately 2,000 tons of goods a year to their Helena stores. Snell & Co., brick makers from Sun River, moved to Fort Benton that spring, too. They were the firm that produced the material for the new brick schoolhouse, another first for Fort Benton. I. G. Baker & Company participated in the building boom when it remodeled some of its store space to provide banking services.[27]

Part of Fort Benton's growth in 1877 was due to the fact that the city and merchants of Helena finally accepted Fort Benton as the head of navigation of the Missouri and therefore, one of the Territory's most vital supply centers. For several years, Helena merchants tried to bypass Fort Benton when it came to securing supplies. Initially, Helena placed its hopes in the Union Pacific Railroad's line to Corinne with an additional 500-mile wagon road connection to Helena. The old Corinne Trail through Utah proved much too slow and cumbersome, however, especially when the river was running high. Steamboats up the Missouri were still the best value in freight rates and time in good seasons.[28]

For a brief moment in 1875, the city of Helena thought that it had finally succeeded in bypassing Fort Benton for good. Low water during the 1874 season made getting boats all the way to Fort Benton problematic—but boats were managing to get as far as the mouth of the Musselshell River. Helena merchants and the Diamond R Transportation Company backed the founding of the town of Carroll, at that location, to serve as a freight landing for the steamboats and as the beginning of a new wagon trail across the Judith Basin to Helena. The Diamond R did a lively business in both 1874 and 1875 working with the Kountz and Coulson Line steamers. In 1875, Sanford Coulson was so confident of Carroll supplanting Fort Benton that his steamers began a weekly packet service between Carroll and Bismarck. The Helena merchants supported the Carroll venture because the new route brought freight to Helena ten days sooner than the usual Fort Benton route. The Carroll experiment, however, was short-lived. When high water returned in 1876, steamboat operators just bypassed the little village on their way to Fort Benton. After 1876, if boats could not reach Fort Benton due to low water, they dropped their freight at Cow Island, 60 miles above Carroll and just below the rapids.[29]

By July 1, 1877, when the *Red Cloud* left Bismarck for a second trip to Fort Benton, the little river town was once again solidly established as the most important commercial center in the Territory. The local paper reported that, "The new steamer *Red Cloud* got off with a fine load, and should

Table 4.3. Manifest of the steamboat *Red Cloud*
July 13, 1877, Bismarck to Fort Benton

L. Lewis, Camp Baker	1 bale carpet
Geo. Stewart	19 packages household goods
I. G. Baker & Co., Battleford	73 packages merchandise
I. G. Baker & Co., Fort Walsh	281 packages merchandise
I. G. Baker & Co., Fort Macleod	322 packages merchandise
I. G. Baker & Co., Fort Benton	4,149 packages merchandise

Benton Weekly Record, July 13, 1877

Table 4.4. Manifest of the steamboat *Red Cloud* July 18, 1877, Fort Benton to Bismarck

J. K. P. Miller, Minneapolis, Minn.	5 boxes merchandise
G. H. Jackson, Egmonsville, Canada	1 box raw furs
W. H. Frank, Bowling Green, Ky.	1 box merchandise
Cassills, Stimson & Co., Montreal, Canada	1 box raw furs
J. & A. Boskowits, Chicago, Ill.	558 dry hides, 152 bales buffalo robes, 98 bales assorted skins
Hartman & Williamson, St. Louis, Mo.	76 bales assorted skins
I. G. Baker & Co., St. Louis, Mo.	23 bales buffalo robes, 24 bales assorted skins
Pope Cole & Co., Baltimore, Md.	298 bags ore
Coats Bros., Philadelphia, Pa.	116 bags wool
Harding, Gray & Dewey, Boston, Mass.	200 bags wool, 10 bales sheep skins

Bismarck Semi-Weekly Tribune, July 18, 1877

make a quick trip as she will have a fine stage of water, and Capt. Massie knows how to handle her."[30] On July 11, the *Red Cloud* arrived at Fort Benton having traveled from Bismarck in 9 days, 23 hours, and 45 minutes—18 hours and 45 minutes less than ever documented before—her first record for speed.[31] The boat brought 175 tons of freight and 15 passengers to Fort Benton.[32] From that time, the *Red Cloud* was noted as one of the fastest Mountain packets on the river and a favorite with passengers because of her speed.[33] On the evening of July 12 the *Red Cloud* headed once again for Bismarck loaded with passengers and freight.[34]

On July 20, with the hold full, the steamer left Bismarck once again for its final trip of the season to Fort Benton. Fort Buford reported to the Bismarck newspaper "that the *Red Cloud* came into port at 11:30 A.M., on the 22nd. The smiling countenance of our old friend 'Gov. Wise' has an unusually happy expression, as with that index finger of his he pointed out to us a place in big letters which read thusly: 'Two (2) days and fifteen hours from Bismarck'; beat it if you can."[35] Obviously the crew of the *Red Cloud* was confident that the boat's reputation for speed would win the day. Captain Wise's faith in his vessel was well founded. The *Red Cloud*'s trip from Bismarck to Fort Benton set the all-time record for speed between those points, 8 days and 17 hours. The boat arrived with twenty-eight passengers and 150 tons of freight consisting of 2,967 packages for I. G. Baker & Company and a wagon for a local man.[36] The boat headed back downriver, arriving in Bismarck on August 7, with sixty passengers and a large consignment of robes, hides, and furs for eastern markets.[37]

Table 4.5. Manifest of the steamboat *Red Cloud* August 7, 1877, Fort Benton to Bismarck

L. Buck	1 box merchandise, 1 chest
Thomas G. Mitchell	1 bale buffalo robes, 1 sewing machine, 5 boxes H H goods
J. J. Kennedy	56 head of cattle, 1 horse
NPRR	2 boxes merchandise, 2 bales elk and deer horns, 443 bales buffalo robes, 59 bales antelope skins, 45 bales deer skins, 2 bales elk skins, 6 bales wolf skins, 4 bales coyote skins, 9 bales beaver skins, 2 bales fine furs, 8 bales kit fox furs, 2 bales skunk furs, 4 bales furs sacked, 5 bales calf skins, 1 bale moose skins, 1 bale badger skins, 144 bags of wool, 1 bale sheep pelts, 176 dry hides

Bismarck Semi-Weekly Tribune, August 8, 1877

Table 4.6. Payments of the North-West Mounted Police to I. G. Baker & Company 1875-77*

	1875-76	*1876-77*
Pay of the force	$18,481.98	—
Subsistence	30,438.29	$38,124.94
Clothing and uniforms	2,608.75	4,685.05
Arms and ammunition	27.91	24.50
Traveling and expenses	598.94	33.50
Freight and transport	4,018.21	3,084.34
Horses and equipment	6,850.02	2,801.23
Forage, etc.	31,428.25	64,435.02
Sleighs, wagons, buggies	406.42	369.49
Buildings and repairs	4,591.91	—
Oxen, carts, harness	127.62	—
Printing, stationary	287.00	116.87
Barrack and camp equipment	2,877.96	3,306.60
Fuel and Light	1,104.75	1,493.80
Telegrams	208.97	—
Postages	57.29	—
Blacksmith stores	707.92	1,066.48
Hospital expenses and stores	1,342.32	272.24
General stores	6,951.14	4,123.69
Rents	49.46	—
Farming implements	1,887.92	93.00
Legal expenses	7,718.82	26.25
Totals	$122,771.85	$122,057.00

*This listing first appeared in the Sessional Papers No. 188, 42 Victoria A 1879 and was reprinted in Berry, *The Whoop-Up Trail,* 66.

Figure 4.2. Steamboats at the Bismarck levee including the *Eclipse* and the *Red Cloud*, n.d. Murphy Library, University of Wisconsin–La Crosse (photograph no. 26811).

The 1877 season proved quite remarkable. Newspapers across the upper Missouri region reported that the Missouri and its tributary trade above Bismarck was "becoming simply enormous"; the growing settlement and occupation of the Yellowstone, Big Horn, Powder, and other valleys that provided markets and products in mining and agriculture along the rivers literally swelled steamboat traffic.[38] Although not quite matching the volume of the glory days of the 1860s, 1877 was a robust commercial year. The steamboat stock alone doubled just to keep up with demand; twenty-five steamboat arrivals were logged for the year, dropping an amazing 5,300 tons of freight at the levee. I. G. Baker & Company and the steamboat *Red Cloud* had a very fine first season on the Missouri River. In the

3-year period 1875–77, I. G. Baker & Company shipped an estimated 1 million pounds of freight to Canada worth $268,224. Its Fort Benton competitor and sometime partner, T. C. Power & Brother, shipped an additional 500,000 pounds of freight.[39] With swelling commercial markets and the continual flow of immigrants coming up the Missouri River, the steamboat business and Fort Benton experienced a third boom.

The town was bustling so much, in fact, that toward the end of the year W. H. Buck, editor of the *Benton Weekly Record,* called for additional town improvements for the next year. Buck suggested the town needed a fire marshal, a new courthouse, a new church, an army post on or near the Milk River to protect Montana from the Canadian Sioux (Fort Assiniboine was built in 1879), a railroad from Fort Benton to Helena, and more of those fabulous brick buildings. After all, Fort Benton's enterprise was on the upswing in 1877: L. H. Rosencranz brought a new saddle and harness business in, there was a new blacksmith, along with a wheelwright, watchmaker, tailor, cobbler, and barber—all hanging shingles in a newly robust Fort Benton.[40]

Even property prices reflected the growth and success of the little river community. Town lots that once were up for the taking were selling for an average of $10 a square foot for Front Street properties. An offer of $1,800 was turned down for an old log home situated near the levee.[41] If editor Buck's predictions were correct, prices would only climb higher in 1878.

5

Fortune Building on the High Plains

> I shall never forget that eleven weeks on the Missouri River with its pleasant associations. There was dancing in the main cabin at night, with violins and guitars for music (there was no piano aboard), square dances for the most part with the waltz another favorite.
>
> —Lou Stocking Stewart, remembrance, 1937

Despite her 1877 success in the Mountain trade, the *Red Cloud* was not well adapted to the shallows of the upper Missouri River. The vessel was long and narrow and drew too much water for late season freighting.[1] During the winter of 1877–78, Baker & Company had the *Red Cloud* lengthened by 50 feet, her guards were removed, and some modifications may have been made to the vessel's bow structure, all with the intent of increasing both the boat's speed and carrying capacity.[2] The newly remodeled steamer was launched from St. Louis on March 12, 1878, and it was reported that with the new modifications the boat drew only 20 inches empty, and, with 100 tons of freight, it drew the same water as it did the previous year when empty; a rousing success was predicted.[3] The new Baker Bonded Line offered through tickets for the 1878 season from Helena to St. Paul, Minnesota, via the *Red Cloud* and the leased *Nellie Peck* on the Missouri,[4] then connecting with the Northern Pacific Railroad (NPRR) at Bismarck, for $70 a trip, first class. This was a solid bargain, as NPRR was advertising $105 for a direct trip from Helena to Omaha, and T. C. Power's Benton Transportation Company was offering its first-class fares for $82.50 from Chicago to Fort Benton. The *Benton Weekly Record* warned travelers that the

Figure 5.1. I. G. Baker & Company freight outfit in front of the *Record* building, n.d. Montana Historical Society, Helena (photograph no. 947-074).

fare from St. Paul to Chicago, St. Louis, New York, and other eastern cities was lower than from Omaha to the same points. Besides, "you could not beat the accommodations offered by the boats of the Baker Line."[5]

All of Fort Benton was ready for the arrival of the first steamers, including the *Red Cloud,* when spring finally came in 1878. The opening of the freighting season saw Fort Benton bustling like never before. Benton's four biggest merchants, T. C. Power & Brother, I. G. Baker & Company, Murphy, Neel and Company, and Helena's Kleinschmidt & Brothers all operated several wagon trains in 1878 and were anxious to see the season's freight arrive. Each of these businesses handled at least 2,000 tons of freight per year. The Power and Baker firms were most fortunate, as they kept their transportation costs to a minimum by using their own steamers for the Missouri River portion of their freighting. Murphy, Neel and Company contracted with the Yankton based Coulson Line, while Kleinschmidt & Brothers relied on contracts with the Kountz steamers. With four large mercantile firms all running freight into Fort Benton on four different steamboat lines, the Fort Benton levee was a busy place in 1878.[6]

Thomas Power, in fact, was betting heavily that the 1878 freighting season would be quite profitable. In April, the *Benton Weekly Record* boasted that Power's Benton Transportation Company (Block P) had contracted for Montana delivery of general merchandise at a lower rate than the Diamond R and the Union Pacific could manage across the old Corinne Trail.[7] The Power firm further positioned itself when it partnered with William Rowe to get the Benton-Helena stage up and running.[8] Finally, after three years of speculation, there was no doubt that Fort Benton had recovered from the economic backslide of the early 1870s. By the time the first steamers reached the levee in the spring, Fort Benton was ready.

The *Red Cloud* was expected to be the first boat to arrive at Fort Benton in 1878. The boat, however, was slower than expected. The steamer was delayed several days after damaging her newly modified hull when she drifted into a bank near St. Joseph, Missouri. She damaged her hull a second time just above Omaha.[9] The steamer also struggled with the typical problems of early season low water. The boat was further delayed on a bar above Sioux City and forced to lighten its load to get over, but the experienced Captain Massie saved considerable time when he paid a local farmer to transport the unloaded freight upriver about a mile by wagon.[10] The newly lengthened *Red Cloud* appeared for the first time at the Fort Benton levee on May 17, 1878, carrying 250 tons of freight and 120 passengers.[11] Captain William Massie reported that her buoyancy was much improved.[12]

In addition to its river freighting, I. G. Baker & Company also found

Table 5.1. Manifest of the steamboat *Red Cloud*
May 17, 1878, St. Louis to Fort Benton

H. A. Page, Virginia City	4 packages
D. Floweree, Helena	3 bull calves, 2 heifer calves
W. S. Wetzel, Benton	10 packages
J. T. Fant, Helena	3 packages
J. L. Perkins, Sun River	1 box
R. S. Ford, Sun River	1 box
J. J. Ellis, Sun River	4 packages
W. H. Marshall, Benton	5 packages
S. C. Ashby, Helena	19 packages
A. B. Hamilton, Benton	1 top buggy
R. S. Hale & Co., Helena	313 packages
Kinna & Jack, Butte City	182 packages
Kinna & Jack, Helena	405 packages
I. G. Baker & Co., Fort Walsh, Canada	512 packages
I. G. Baker & Co., Fort Edmonton, Canada	6 packages
I. G. Baker & Co., Fort Calgary, Canada	6 packages
I. G. Baker & Co., Fort McLeod, Canada	366 packages
I. G. Baker & Co., Fort Benton, Mont.	3,000 packages

Benton Weekly Record, April 26, and May 17, 1878

itself heavily involved in the Canadian beef business in 1878. From 1874 to 1877 the North-West Mounted Police (NWMP) managed to get most of its meat supply from the local buffalo herds. By 1878, however, the number of buffalo in and around the Canadian prairies was greatly diminished by over-hunting. By the mid-1870s, rumors that the American government was paying a bounty of $3 per buffalo robe had taken its toll on the buffalo population. It was reported that the American government rationalized the widespread buffalo slaughter by promoting the belief that the destruction of the buffalo herds would eliminate the problem of getting American Indians to settle on reservations. Although there was no real bounty as an incentive, mass destruction of the herds took place anyway. Historian Gerald Berry suggested that the robe trade from forts Walsh and Macleod fell from nearly 50,000 robes in 1877 to 30,999 in 1878, to 14,000 in 1879, and to only a few hundred by 1880.[13]

To make up for the lack of locally available meat, the NWMP contracted with Baker & Company to furnish the force with domestic beef herded up from Montana and other locations along the Missouri. The contract price for the beef was 14 cents a pound, providing Baker & Company a huge profit margin considering it only paid $20 a head for the cattle in Montana

Figure 5.2. The Fort Benton levee, 1878. National Archives of Canada, Ottawa (photograph no. C19038A).

Table 5.2. Manifest of the steamboat *Red Cloud* June 9, 1878, Bismarck to Fort Benton

I. G. Baker & Co., Fort Benton	1,267 packages—1,267 lbs.
I. G. Baker & Co., Fort Walsh, Canada	285 packages—30,280 lbs.
Major Walsh, Fort Walsh	1 package—20 lbs.
R. Scott, Fort Walsh	1 packages—40 lbs.
I. G. Baker & Co., Fort McLeod, Canada	541 packages—52,670 lbs.
Samuel Horner, Fort McLeod	1 package—10 lbs.
J. H. McKnigh & Co., Fort Shaw, Mont.	2 packages—100 lbs.
Kinna & Jack, Helena	1,419 packages—142,800 lbs.
C. L. Vawter & Co., Helena	337 packages—160,470 lbs.
J. W. Hathaway, Helena	1 package—130 lbs.
E. Lounsbury, Helena	2 packages—160 lbs.
L. Sieben & Bro., Helena	1 package—70 lbs.
Loeb Bros., Helena	16 packages—930 lbs.
M. S. Gibbs, Helena	4 packages—600 lbs.
R. S. Hale & Co., Helena	600 packages—46,000 lbs.
O. G. Birdseye, Blackfoot City	34 packages—4,120 lbs.
R. L. May, Bozeman	20 packages—2,560 lbs.

Benton Weekly Record, June 14, 1878

and only slightly more if the cattle were shipped upriver via steamboat.[14] In addition to supplying beef for the NWMP, I. G. Baker & Company was also responsible for supplying the Canadian government with beef to fill its treaty obligations with the Blackfeet.[15] David Breen of the University of British Columbia estimated that by late 1878 and 1879, the Canadian government's beef contracts with I. G. Baker & Company alone were worth more than $500,000 per year.[16]

While Isaac Baker and the Conrad brothers were getting into the cattle business, the *Red Cloud* made its second arrival of 1878 at the Fort Benton levee. After first dropping sixty recruits for the Canadian North-West Mounted Police at the mouth of the Marias River, the boat landed in Fort Benton on June 9 with fifty-five passengers including Colonel Fred White, Canada's assistant secretary of state, and Major Walsh of the Canadian North-West Mounted Police,[17] and 281 tons of freight.[18] The *Red Cloud* was quickly loaded for the downriver trip and left Fort Benton for Bismarck on June 11 with a heavy load of cattle and other freight bound for eastern markets.[19]

On June 21, the *Red Cloud* made its third arrival of the 1878 season at Fort Benton, but unlike all the previous trips, this time it was with Captain

Table 5.3. Manifest of the steamboat *Red Cloud* June 11, 1877, Fort Benton to Bismarck

U.S. Express Co.	1 box
Peter Seims	21 head of cattle
Henry C. King	15 bales sacks
NPRR	18 boxes merchandise, 2 trunks, 1 chest, 47 bales sheep pelts, 298 buffalo robes, 47 bales assorted furs, 3 boxes assorted furs, 8 bales calf skins, 187 beef hides

Bismarck Tri-Weekly Tribune, June 21, 1878

Table 5.4. Manifest of the steamboat *Red Cloud* July 5, 1878, Bismarck to Fort Benton

J. E. Wenerd	1 package—200 lbs.
S. P Wolcott	10 packages—650 lbs.
W. G. Conrad	1 package—320 lbs.
H. H. Wells	3 packages—700 lbs.
H. A. Hanry	4 packages—640 lbs.
Kinna & Jack	294 packages—25,860 lbs.
J. Denn	263 packages—12,800 lbs.
C. L. Vawter	2,925 packages—254,900 lbs.
I. G. Baker & Co., Fort Benton	3,094 packages—285,510 lbs.

Benton Weekly Record, July 5, 1878

Paul Murphy in command. The famed Captain Massie had left the *Red Cloud* to use his knowledge of the Missouri River on another boat.[20] The steamer arrived in Fort Benton on July 5 with 260 tons of freight.[21]

By the time the 1878 freighting season was over, the *Red Cloud* had off-loaded 981 tons of freight near Fort Benton and had brought 360 passengers into the Fort Benton area.[22] Although a huge success, 1878 was not without setbacks for the *Red Cloud.* In July, the steamer broke her paddle-wheel shaft about 80 miles above Bismarck (near the mouth of the Little Missouri River) while up-bound for Fort Benton. Her passengers were transferred to the *Josephine* and her freight to the *General Terry.* After the boat limped back to Bismarck, the shaft was removed and shipped by rail to Chicago for welding repairs.[23] Repairs would not be completed, however, in time for the steamer to make another trip to Fort Benton before low water set in for the season. The *Red Cloud* did, however, manage to drop freight at Cow Island on August 22 and September 27, after her repair work was completed.

In 1878, the Baker Line expanded when the tiny steamer *Colonel Macleod* was added to its Mountain fleet.[24] The *Colonel Macleod* was a sternwheel packet, 196 feet by 26 feet, with an iron paddle-wheel with wooden buckets; the boat was rated at just 110 tons. The steamer was built by C. T. Dumont of Cincinnati, Ohio, and was named for the assistant commissioner of the Canadian North-West Mounted Police. The steamer operated between Fort Benton and Bismarck during the regular season and then was used as a shuttle for freight left at Cow Island (due to low water) late in the season. Larger packets like the *Red Cloud* and the *Nellie Peck* often left freight at Cow Island rather than risk the low water between Cow Island and Fort Benton. Running the *Colonel Macleod* from Cow Island to Fort Benton often extended the supply season from early September well into October and allowed the Baker Line to remain competitive during low water seasons.[25] The *Colonel Macleod* made the first of many appearances at the Fort Benton levee on August 29, 1878, carrying forty passengers and 110

Figure 5.3. Freight trains leaving Fort Benton loaded for the Whoop-Up Trail, 1878. National Archives of Canada, Ottawa (photograph no. C19038B).

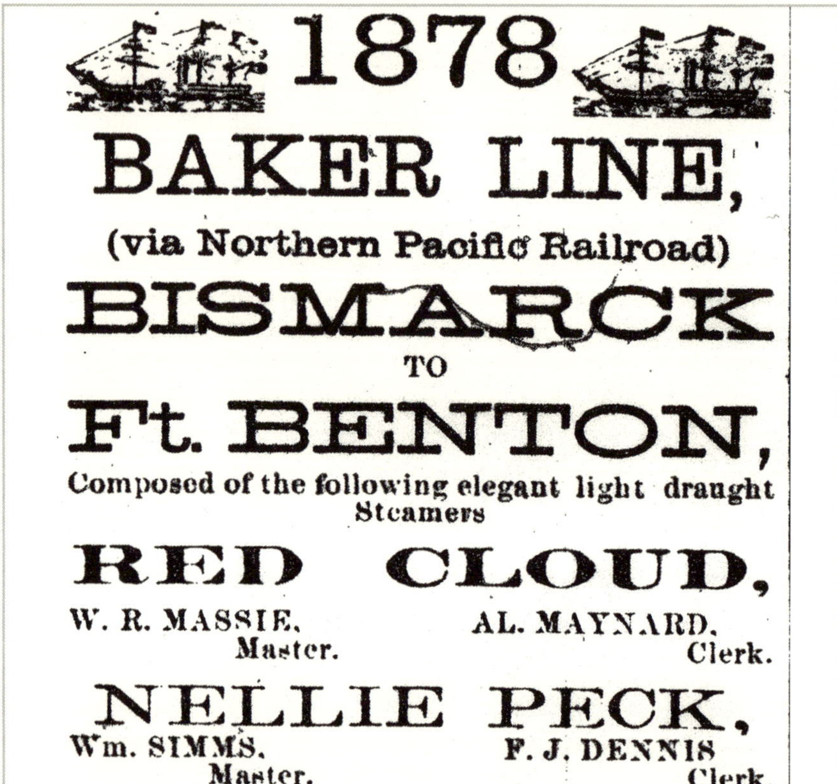

Figure 5.4. Advertisement for the steamers of the Baker Line, 1878. *Bismarck Tribune,* May 24, 1878.

tons of freight. The boat finally headed downriver to winter in Bismarck on October 21, after successfully extending the Fort Benton freighting season by several weeks.[26]

I. G. Baker & Company's steamers, *Red Cloud, Colonel Macleod,* and the leased *Nellie Peck,* helped bring an estimated total of 9,400 tons of freight to Fort Benton and more than 1,400 passengers in 1878. A staggering fifty-one arrivals were logged at the levee. Headed back downriver were approximately four hundred passengers and roughly 75,000 buffalo robes—striking proof that the herds were indeed being decimated. T. C. Power reported shipping 25,000 robes and Baker & Company shipped another 20,000. Thirty thousand of the estimated 75,000 robes shipped for the year were reportedly coming from the Whoop-Up country and the Cypress Hills region of Canada.[27]

Financially, 1878 was a huge success for I. G. Baker & Company. The firm succeeded in shipping $2.5 million worth of freight through Fort Benton, making the firm the single largest taxpayer in Montana that year.[28]

6

Freight, Freight, and More Freight, 1879–81

As for cargo, I might compare this trip of the "Red Cloud" to that of Noah's ark. We had aboard almost everything one could enumerate in the way of livestock—cattle, horses, mules, pigs, chickens, ducks and turkeys. Over my stateroom was chained a big Newfoundland dog that kept me awake nights by dragging his chain about.

—Lou Stocking Stewart, remembrance, 1937

The *Red Cloud* spent the winter of 1879 in St. Louis where it was slightly overhauled. With the news that ice upriver had begun to break, the steamer left St. Louis on March 25. The boat had a difficult voyage. The river was plagued with shoal water, heavy ice, mountain floods, and adverse winds. In charge that season was Captain John A. Williams with L. L. Hines as clerk, Ben Jewell and Jacob Faux as pilots, A. B. Bone and D. Smith as engineers, Charles Detz as mate, and Frank Norris serving as steward.[1] On May 11 the *Red Cloud* arrived at Fort Benton with a cargo of 349 tons of freight, which included horses, mules, sheep, and cattle. The vessel also carried 215 Canadian Mounties for the northern territory, and 150 others.[2] The passenger list also included ten members of the Gardner family who were moving to Montana from Missouri.[3] The steamer was loaded and headed back downriver to Bismarck on May 13 with 26 passengers and a considerable freight that demonstrated the efforts of trappers and hunters in the region. In addition to the usual bales of buffalo robes, the steamer carried antelope, deer, sheep, elk, skunk, kit fox, muskrat, lynx, badger, beaver, wolf, and cow hides.

The *Red Cloud* was quite busy in the early season. It left Bismarck for

Table 6.1. Manifest of the steamboat *Red Cloud* May 13, 1879, Fort Benton to Bismarck

Quarter Master stores for Coal Banks	9,735 lbs.
I. G. Baker & Co., St. Louis, Mo.	720 bales buffalo robes (61,165 lbs.), 3 boxes merchandise (475 lbs.), 17 bales antelope (1,475 lbs.), 18 bales deer (1,789 lbs.), 1 bale sheep (169 lbs.), 1 bale elk (170 lbs.), 4 bales skunk (569 lbs.), 2 bales kit fox (300 lbs.), 11 bales musk rat (879 lbs.), 1 bale lynx (104 lbs.), 6 bales badger (938 lbs.), 13 bales beaver (1,132 lbs.), 9 bales wolf (900 lbs.), 50 beef hides (1,250 lbs.)

Benton Weekly Record, May 16, 1879

Fort Benton on May 26 with two notable passengers on board. One was the notorious newspaperman, Stanley Huntley, who reportedly interviewed Sitting Bull for the *Chicago Tribune,*[4] and the other was Assistant Commissioner James Macleod of the North-West Mounted Police, who was escorting a fresh crop of new recruits for the force.[5] The trip was delayed near the mouth of the Yellowstone River while a large herd of buffalo crossed.

The *Red Cloud* arrived at the Fort Benton levee on June 9 with thirty-nine passengers, and 319 tons of freight,[6] after first dropping one hundred Canadian Mounted Police and seventy-six horses at Coal Banks.[7] When the steamer arrived at Fort Benton that June, she found the river community bustling like never before.

Just as editor Buck had predicted, 1879 looked like a robust year for Fort Benton and her leading merchants. Three new large buildings went up in town: W. H. Buck and his *Record* finally got their three-story brick building; T. C. Power & Brother completed the first half of what would be a two-story brick store; and, not to be outdone by its chief rival, I. G. Baker & Company put up a slightly larger building for its enterprise. Construction all over Fort Benton proceeded rapidly. Paris Gibson opened a fully stocked lumber yard in June, only to sell out his entire inventory just six weeks later.[8]

The *Red Cloud* made two more trips to Fort Benton in 1879, arriving on July 4 and 24. It once again had a successful season moving freight to and from Fort Benton for I. G. Baker & Company and others.[9] In addition to the loads carried by the *Red Cloud,* the Baker Line's little steamer, the *Colonel Macleod,* hauled freight and extended the season well into September. In

Figure 6.1. Handbill advertising the Baker Line of steamers. Joel F. Overholser Historical Research Center, Schwinden Library and Archives, Fort Benton, Montana.

Table 6.2. Manifest of the steamboat *Red Cloud*
June 9, 1879, Bismarck to Fort Benton

I. G. Baker & Co., Fort Benton	1,646 packages
Paul Gibson	3 packages
Thos. Cummings	2 packages
W. Berkfield	55 packages
W. Windor	1 package
Chas Lehman	485 packages
C. Boissenault	24 packages
Paynter, Brown & Co.	250 packages
R. Pellet & Co.	87 packages
R. S. Ford	3 packages
Fred Lehman	700 packages
L. H. Osborne	1 package
R. T. May & Co.	13 packages
T. C. Rooselvelt	10 packages
J. F. Porter	21 packages
Wetzel & Co.	35 packages
E. J. Birdseye	8 packages
Davis & Tatem	20 tons iron and 16 packages machinery
Hershberg & Nathan	2 packages
Shaffer & Co.	69 packages
Auerbach, Wells & Co.	538 packages
G. C. Boose	17 packages
I. G. Baker & Co.	15 packages
W. C. Zook	1 package
A. M. Holter	52 packages
J. K. Weston	1 package
John Beckney	15 packages
W. G. Conrad	3 packages
Col. Macleod	38 packages, 76 head of horses

Benton Weekly Record, June 13, 1879

fact, in 1879 steamboat traffic on the upper Missouri River reached its highest point ever with forty-seven steamboat arrivals at Fort Benton. Altogether, these vessels carried approximately 9,444 tons of freight upriver. I. G. Baker & Company's *Red Cloud* brought in almost 25 percent of the freight to Fort Benton that year (2,015 tons).[10]

The heavy freighting upriver and the large downriver shipments of skins and hides on the *Red Cloud* early in the season had a few adverse results for I. G. Baker & Company, however. In late summer the firm had difficulty filling orders for calfskins and buffalo robes to be used in the fall for making coats for local consumption. Greenhood, Bohm & Company, a

Figure 6.2. Bull train leaving Fort Benton hauling freight into the Whoop-Up country. National Archives of Canada, Ottawa (photograph no. C43142).

clothier in Helena, and the NWMP had to wait until September for its coat orders to be filled.[11] Likewise, the Montana Steam Cracker Company, of Bozeman, had to wait for the *Colonel Macleod* to reach Fort Benton in late September before Baker & Company could ship its goods to market.[12] The delays demonstrated that in 1879 commerce on the Montana plains was still solidly dependent on Missouri River transportation.

In addition to carrying substantial local and Canadian freight, I. G. Baker & Company also won the U.S. Military contract in 1879 to transport freight by wagon from Cow Island to posts along the interior; winning this contract further solidified I. G. Baker & Company as a major competitor for regional transportation. Baker & Company would continue to bid and win wagon transportation contracts for the U.S. government for several years to come.[13]

One truly unfortunate event befell the Baker Line in 1879. On November 18, the firm's little steamer, the *Colonel Macleod,* was destroyed in Bismarck when the T. C. Power & Brother steamer, the *Butte,* slipped off its stays and crushed the smaller boat. It was unfortunate for I. G. Baker & Company to lose such a useful boat, doubly so given the fact that the incident resulted in a long court battle between the Baker and Power firms over recovering damages and associated libel charges.[14]

Despite the unfortunate loss of the *Colonel Macleod* for both the community and Baker & Company, 1879 was a successful freighting and building year. Economically the city and its merchants did quite well. By the early fall, the city completed a new courthouse on Main Street. George Crane opened a variety store, and Hirshberg & Nathan opened a clothing store in the busy river town. Government engineers finally began work to improve the channel conditions of the Missouri River; they removed an estimated 5,000 rocks at Dauphin's Rapids, and four newly installed wing dams deepened the channel by almost 12 inches. The engineers' effort was an act both pushed for and applauded by every working steamboat pilot in the Territory. A promising discovery of gold was made in the Judith Basin in August, and in October Fort Benton's first legal hanging took place.[15] There seemed to be no end in sight to the progress at hand.

Freight and Remembrance, 1880

I. G. Baker & Company once again won the contract to supply the Canadian North-West Mounted Police in 1880. That same year, the Conrad brothers and Isaac G. Baker established the Circle cattle ranch in Canada to take advantage of the firms renewed beef contracts.[16] The *Red Cloud* was the primary vehicle scheduled to carry the Canadian trade; consequently, 1880 looked to be another fine year for the Baker Line.

Fortunately, one of the boat's 1880 passengers left an intimate account of her journey on the steamboat *Red Cloud*, providing valuable insight (see Appendix A for the full transcription). The passenger was Lou Stocking [Stewart], an early resident of Fort Benton, Montana. She first arrived there in July 1865. Her father owned a meat market and later established a ranch along Teton Creek, on which Lou grew up. In 1910, she married Albert H. Stewart. They lived in and around Fort Benton and Great Falls, Montana, for many years. Stocking was a prolific writer, keeping extensive diaries and later in life writing summaries about her life in Montana.[17] Her comments concerning her journey up the Missouri River on the *Red Cloud* and the freight that the boat carried adds support to the notion that Fort Benton had become, by 1880, the freighting mecca on the Great Plains. Lou wrote in her journal:

> As for the cargo, I might compare this trip of the "Red Cloud" to that of Noah's ark. We had aboard almost everything one could enumerate in the way of livestock—cattle, horses, mules, pigs, chickens, ducks and turkeys. Over my stateroom was chained a big Newfoundland dog that

Figure 6.3. Front Street and steamboat landing, Fort Benton, n.d.

> kept me awake nights by dragging his chain about. Then there was the usual tonnage of foodstuff, mainly salt pork, bacon and flour which was to be distributed at different towns along the river.[18]

Ms. Stewart's account provides detail of steamboat life that is rarely reported elsewhere. It is odd, however, that given all that she chronicled about her steamboat journey, her account does not mention the fact that the *Red Cloud,* on this first journey of the 1880 season, lost its starboard smokestack when a guide-wire gave way as the boat was passing under the Union Pacific Bridge at Sioux City. The stack reportedly came crashing to the main deck with quite a force.[19] One might wonder where Ms. Stewart was when such a racket was created on the boat. Nonetheless, Ms. Stewart's account is a fine example of what it was like to travel as a cabin passenger on a Missouri River steamer. Few accounts with this detail exist today.

When the *Red Cloud* and Ms. Stewart arrived at Fort Benton, a large cargo of bulls, thoroughbred rams, carriages, and other supplies linked to Montana's growing livestock industry was unloaded.[20] The *Red Cloud* headed back downriver to Bismarck on June 18 with another diverse hide freight and seventeen passengers. The boat arrived in Bismarck on June 25.[21]

Montana Historical Society, Helena (photograph no. 947-051).

Just like the previous season, when the *Red Cloud* arrived at Fort Benton, the steamer found an ever-busy frontier town. The local newspapers reported that Montana Territory's population was growing by leaps and bounds. Business over the past five years spurred growth throughout the area. The 1870 territorial population of 20,595 almost doubled by 1880 when the decennial census reported the population as 39,159. Fort Benton was the third largest community in the Territory in 1870, with 1,618 citizens—only Helena and Butte were larger.[22]

The population increase meant more business for the whole Territory. As always, the railroad barons were anxious to try to cut out the Missouri River business. On March 9, 1880, the Utah Northern Railroad drove its first spike. When the first rails were laid in Montana Territory, it caused barely a quiver for those communities hoping to be along the rail line. Steel rails in southwestern Montana meant little to bustling Fort Benton as long as the river ran high. Although the volume of overland freight between the new railhead and Helena was significantly less than the old Corinne Trail, it was still farther to Helena from the railhead than it was from Fort Benton. It was still faster and cheaper to use the river, a lesson that past experience had taught the Helena merchants.[23]

Table 6.3. Manifest of the steamboat *Red Cloud* June 10, 1880, St. Louis to Fort Benton

I. A. Hodson	523 packages
Hampton & Wetzel	148 packages
I. G. Baker & Co.	3,711 packages, 1 wagon
Jos. A Baker	68 packages, 3 bulls
A. J. Smith	64 packages
J. L. Perkins	111 packages
C. Tool	14 packages
George A. Baker	19 packages, 3 rams
C. Clark & Curtin	265 packages, 1 carriage
R. Payne	5 packages
A. A. Martin	9 packages
W. B. Eagan	43 packages
Chas. Blackburn	11 packages
Dr. Greenlee	2 packages
R. S. Ford	10 packages
W. L. Stocking	7 packages
M. Farrell	12 packages
C. W. Price	28 packages
S. Hauser	1 package
I. E. Brooks	12 packages
L. Knouse	2 packages
Joe Patterson	1 package
Mrs. E. Berry	22 packages
Mr. Harrison	5 packages
A. Walston	2 packages
Mrs. A. Wilston	2 packages
H. King	5 packages
A. G. Clark	69 packages
China Clark	67 packages
M. Cullen	53 packages
J. S. Rice	65 packages
E. Willson	65 packages
J. Seifert	35 packages
I. A. Woodson	8 mares, 4 mules, 2 wagons, 3 carriages
Mr. Berry	2 horses
M. Harrison	2 mules
Mr. Lemas	8 heifers
A. Watson	4 mules
P. P. Broad	2 colts
A. Freeze	2 horses
E. Toole	2 wagons
W. B. Eagan	1 wagon
Caplice & Smith	1 coach

Table 6.3. (*continued*)

Mr. Harrison	1 wagon
A. Walton	2 wagons
J. L. Rice	1 phaeton
W. Seifert	1 wagon
E. Wilson	1 carriage

Benton Weekly Record, June 11, 1880

Table 6.4. Manifest of the steamboat *Red Cloud* June 18, 1880, Fort Benton to Bismarck

I. G. Baker & Co., St. Louis	1,471 beef hides, 12 bear skins, 1,050 wolf pelts, 100 badger skins, 500 skunk skins, 2,000 rat skins, 110 elk skins, 250 sheep skins, 4,650 deer skins, 4,000 antelope skins, 4,490 buffalo robes, 100 head of cattle

Benton Weekly Record, June 18, 1880

The Fort Benton levee was as busy as always when the *Red Cloud* returned for the second time of the season. The boat arrived at Fort Benton on July 4, with 450 tons of freight and a number of passengers.[24] The *Red Cloud* returned back downriver on July 7 with a varied assortment of freight and one of the earliest large exports of cattle from Montana by river.[25]

The *Red Cloud*'s final appearance at Fort Benton in 1880 was on July 23. The steamer brought another 350 tons of goods, as a well as thirty more passengers.[26] The boat then returned downriver with another heavy load of cattle.[27] When the freight tab was closed for the month of July, a remarkable 3,000 tons of cargo was left at the levee. The *Red Cloud* and the *Key West* both managed two appearances each in July; adding to the July freight tally were also arrivals by the *Eclipse, Nellie Peck, Helena, Rosebud, Benton, Butte,* and the *C. K. Peck.* Steamboats managed to drop freight at Montana locations well into September in 1880. The *F. Y. Batchelor* closed the far upper river when it dropped its freight at the mouth of the Musselshell on November 12. All told, more than 12,000 tons of freight entered Montana via the Missouri River in 1880. The Utah Northern Railroad shipped just under 10,000 tons, while the Northern Pacific Railroad added another 6,700 tons—once again the Missouri River route proved competitive.[28]

Figure 6.4. Cow Island landing, ca. 1880. Montana Historical Society, Helena (photograph no. H-318).

Politicking and Freighting on the High Plains, 1881

The next season was as successful for I. G. Baker & Company and the *Red Cloud* as previous years. The steamer carried goods not only for Baker & Company and the NWMP but for many Montana businesses, as well. Before the onset of the freighting season T. C. Power & Brother consigned more than 42 tons of goods on the first trip of the *Red Cloud*.[29] The boat arrived at Fort Benton and the surrounding area a total of four times that season and delivered a total of 1,400 tons of freight and several hundred passengers.

In 1881, I. G. Baker & Company once again won the Canadian gov-

Table 6.5. Manifest of the steamboat *Red Cloud*
July 4, 1880, Bismarck to Fort Benton

I. G. Baker & Co., Benton	3,593 packages, 1 car wagons
I. G. Baker & Co., Fort Walsh	329 packages
I. G. Baker & Co., Fort McLeod	149 packages
I. G. Baker & Co., Wood Mountain	39 packages
I. G. Baker & Co., Saskatchewan	9 packages
I. N. Baker	3 packages
W. S. Wetzel, Fort Benton	59 packages
R. M. Renshaw, Butte	23 packages
M. Rening, Helena	1 package
Cassidy & McD.	1 hay press
W. G. Conrad	5 packages
Morse & B., new Chicago	3 packages
R. S. Hale & Co.	1 lot gas pipes
H. Colbert, Helena	12 packages
Clark, Conrad & Curtiss	20 packages
Geo. Berman, Helena	67 packages
Hirshberg & Nathan	2 packages
Hazlett & Hamilton	19 packages
E. Mahan	1 package
I. Auchars, Fort Shaw	1 package
N.W.M.P.	11 packages, 1 stallion
W. J. Hide, McLeod	1 harvester
R. M. McCleichy	1 package
I. W. Peck	21 packages
E. G. Brockey	8 rams
Lt. C. B. Heuton, Fort Logan	2 packages
S. C. Ashby	2 packages
D. Prosser	2 packages
Murphy, Neil & Co.	2 packages
Lt. Bartlett, Fort Logan	1 package
T. Caldwell	1 package
J. C. Nelson	[?]
Owner on board	sheep and 1 horse

Benton Weekly Record, July 9, 1880

ernment contracts.[30] In anticipation of moving more freight than the *Red Cloud* could handle, I. G. Baker & Company made arrangements with T. C. Power's Fort Benton Transportation Company (Block P) boats (the *Benton, Helena, Butte,* and the new *Black Hills*) to carry the firm's surplus freight. Power agreed to extend Baker & Company in-house freight rates on the *Red Cloud* surplus freight: equal to Power and Brother freight on rates and

Table 6.6. Manifest of the steamboat *Red Cloud* July 7, 1880, Fort Benton to Bismarck

I. G. Baker & Co., St. Louis	6 bales assorted furs, 12 bales coyote skins, 19 bales wolf skins, 4 bales badger skins, 21 bales buffalo robes, 1 bale rat skins, 3 bales skunk hides, 5 bales beaver skins, 1 bale kit fox, 10 bales deer skins, 31 bales antelope skins, 1 bale sheep and antelope skins, 8 bales elk skins, 1 bale mountain sheep hides, 1 bale black bear skins, 1 bale fox skins, 1 bale grizzly and black bear skins, 119 beef hides, 180 head of cattle

Benton Weekly Record, July 9, 1880

Table 6.7. Manifest of the steamboat *Red Cloud* July 23, 1880, Bismarck to Fort Benton

I. G. Baker & Co., Benton	3,500 sacks flour, 6 cars lumber, 1 car wagons, 175 packages of groceries
Mrs. Spaulding	19 packages
Sarah Bean	6 packages
Geo. Clendenin	13,000 lbs. meat
J. C. Bailey	44 packages
C. W. Price	14 packages
J. McFarlin	1 thresher
Tom Todd	110 packages
Hirshberg & Nathan	6 packages
W. S. Wetzel	165 packages
NWM Police, Fort McLeod	29 packages
NWM Police, Fort Walsh	32 packages
E. C. Larabie	1 carriage

Benton Weekly Record, July 23, 1880

delivery: 80 cents per 100 pounds for the high water month of June up to a maximum of 900 tons of freight. Rates for June from Bismarck to Coal Banks were guaranteed at 75 cents per 100 pounds. Freight shipped between July 10 and 20 were guaranteed at $1.20 to Fort Benton and $1.00 for Coal Banks; between July 21 and August 1 the rates were $1.95 and $1.75; after August 1 and for the balance of the season the rates were $2.40 to Benton and $1.90 to Coal Banks. In all cases, the freight would be shipped on whichever Block P boat was next available to the desired destination. This was a good arrangement for both companies since it kept the freight rates low (beyond what the *Red Cloud* could carry), and kept the money earned in upper river freighting in the local Fort Benton market rather than letting the money go to downriver companies such as the Kountz or Coulson Lines.[31]

This cooperation between the two companies was not insignificant. By 1881, the competition for the trade in Montana Territory and the Canadian prairies grew fierce as firms outside of Fort Benton began negotiating for shares in the lucrative government markets. It must be remembered that the contracts to provide goods and services to the Canadian and American governments were the major source of income for both I. G. Baker & Company and T. C. Power & Brother.[32] To guarantee their hold on both government trades, the firms struck a remarkable deal of cooperation in January 1881. The two companies agreed not to encroach on each other's trading spheres.[33] Historian Henry Klassen argued, "in practical terms, Power gave Baker every opportunity to secure the Mounted Police and Indian contracts by neither tendering for them nor putting in higher bids. When it came to the U.S. Indian contracts for Montana Territory, Baker reciprocated."[34] The profits each firm received from these contracts was then divided: Power received one-quarter of Baker's returns and Baker received one-quarter of Power's earnings. This agreement reinforced the Baker firm's position as the dominant Fort Benton house in the Canadian prairie region.[35]

By guaranteeing that both firms would support the other's business ventures, both companies insured the maximum profit margin would remain in Fort Benton. The two firms renewed this agreement well into the mid-1880s.[36] T. C. Power & Brother's share of Baker's 1881 Canadian business, for example, was $12,000.[37] Likewise, by cooperating, both firms insured that each firm's steamboats would never have empty cargo holds. As in previous years, the success of both companies depended not only on the ability to win government contracts but also on the ability to maintain their transportation networks.

It was not just the Power and Baker firms that prepared for the upcoming season. Like the previous few years, new businesses opened almost weekly in Fort Benton. Between January and May advertisements for new business ventures were regularly found in the *Benton Weekly Record:* Dutro & Kielhauer were the new stone masons in town; Allen & Tierney added a saloon to Benton; Mrs. Beckman opened a boarding house called the Cosmopolitan Hotel; John Lilly advertised the Lee Isabell Break of Day House, and George Farmer opened the Jungle. W. H. Burgess opened

Fort Benton's first grocery-only store; Gans & Klein clothier moved into a new brick building as did Baker & DeLorimier Home Furnishings. Neil McIntyre opened a boot and shoe shop, and W. J. Minar became the town's newest druggist. The Yankton-based Coulson Steamboat Line even built a brick warehouse in Fort Benton.[38]

Every citizen was ready and waiting for the steamers to come; however, by mid-April there was still no sign of the first boat. The *River Press* reported that excessive high water downriver was holding up the boats.[39] The first boat, the *Far West,* did not arrive until May 19. The *Red Cloud* finally made it to Fort Benton on May 25. The steamer unloaded 250 tons of cargo consigned mainly to I. G. Baker & Company. There were a number of passengers on board including ninety recruits for the Canadian North-West Mounted Police who were landed at Coal Banks.[40]

The *Red Cloud,* a favorite with many Missouri River passengers, was the first choice of the Canadian North-West Mounted Police when the vessel was available. It seems that on this first trip of 1881, the recruits developed an affinity for Mr. P. S. Starr, the boat's first mate. When the boat drew up at Coal Banks for disembarkation, the recruits reportedly gathered around Mr. Starr before their departure to pay tribute (Appendix B) for the fine service they had received, and the whole detachment sang him farewell:

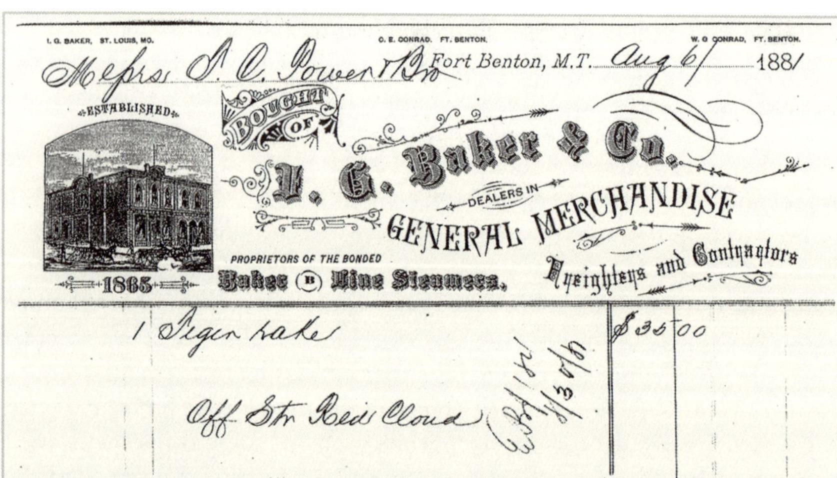
I. G. BAKER, ST. LOUIS, MO. C. E. CONRAD, FT. BENTON. W. G. CONRAD, FT. BENTON.

Messrs. T. C. Power & Bro Fort Benton, M.T. Aug 6 1881

ESTABLISHED 1865

BOUGHT OF I. G. Baker & Co.

DEALERS IN GENERAL MERCHANDISE

PROPRIETORS OF THE BONDED Baker (B) Line Steamers, Freighters and Contractors

1 Tiger rake	$35 00
Off Str Red Cloud	

Figure 6.5. Bill of sale from I. G. Baker & Company to T. C. Power & Brother for the purchase of a Tiger rake carried by the steamboat *Red Cloud.* Montana Historical Society, Helena (Manuscript Collection 55(228-7)).

Figure 6.6. Steamboat *Peninah* at Coal Banks, 1880. Montana Historical Society, Helena (photograph no. H-370).

> Twinkle, twinkle little Star(r), How we'll wonder where you are;
> When from you we're far away, We'll oftimes pause and say, How's our little Starr to-day;
> Is he well or is he ailing—Is he on the "Red Cloud" sailing?
> Is he swearing at "them niggers?" In which trait he often figures, Promising jobs to grave-yard diggers.[41]

Although offensive by today's standards, the song demonstrates the strong tie between the NWMP and the *Red Cloud* and her crew.

Not just a source of great amusement for the NWMP and the people of Benton, the *Red Cloud* and its crew brought cargoes that ranged from the necessary and mundane to the sophisticated and unusual. The spring arrival of the boat and its 3,000 plus packages was a major event for the community. The *Red Cloud* delivered a wide variety of groceries, furniture, hardware, and many fancy goods that soon became the talk of the town. In addition, the boat carried in the largest selection of harness and

Table 6.8. Manifest of the steamboat *Red Cloud* May 25, 1881, St. Louis to Fort Benton

T. C. Power	2 horses
B. I. Rotwell	51 packages
First National Bank	7 packages
T. J. Todd	25 packages
J. R. Wilton	1 package
W. B. Settle, Helena	18 packages
H. M. Young, Helena	7 packages
Mrs. N. Connelly	16 packages
J. M. Ray	17 packages
Joe Baker, Benton	1 package
I. N. Hazlett, Old Agency	6 packages
A. B. Hamilton, Old Agency	1 package
O. H. Morgan, Old Agency	13 packages
Hamilton & Hazlett, Old Agency	168 packages
Clark, Conrad & Curtin	90 packages
Sharp & Graves, Centerville	26 packages
I. G. Baker & Co.	3,271 packages

Benton Weekly Record, June 9, 1881

saddlery ware ever brought to Fort Benton. The local paper suggested that, "no firm in the Northwest carries a more complete stock and deserves more credit for thoroughly upright business dealings" than I. G. Baker & Company.[42]

The citizens of Fort Benton had to settle for the arrival of the *Red Cloud* and a few other boats in the last couple of weeks of May because the June arrivals proved disappointing for everyone. On June 15, the *River Press* explained that it was not an issue of a lack of freight for the season; Bismarck was reporting that, "seven million pounds of freight are in Bismarck awaiting shipment, and the business of the Territory kept lagging therefrom, while a fleet of steamboats are carrying numerous bands of Indians on a Picnic down the Yellowstone."[43] Having been starved out of Canada, bands of refugee Sioux were crossing the border to surrender to the U.S. military at Buford and other posts. Those missing steamboats were transporting Indians to various reservations rather than hauling freight.[44]

In late June, the pace at the levee finally quickened, and Baker store stock again increased with the second arrival of the *Red Cloud* on June 29. Due to the slow start early in the season, and because of the unusual opulence of the *Red Cloud* for a Missouri River steamer (a texas deck and fine staterooms), the boat's arrival was greatly anticipated and colorfully announced that June:

> The smoke from the *Red Cloud*'s smokestacks was seen two hours before sunset last evening, but the night being darker than a stack of black cats and a piece of bad river between her and the Benton wharf, it was contrary to the expectations of our people that the boat pushed through and tied up here last night. With her customary energy, which does not allow a moment to be wasted, the *Red Cloud*, the sparks flying from her smokestacks, came around the bend at eleven o'clock [and] threw out her gang plank.[45]

The steamer unloaded thirty-two passengers and a variety of freight, including a fine assortment of business suits, shirts, and "fine" underwear for the gentlemen of Benton, all of which was soon on display at the I. G. Baker & Company store.[46]

The steamer left Benton and headed back to Bismarck on June 30. The boat took a large group of passengers and freight for Bismarck and cattle purchased from Jack Harris of Highwood for delivery at the Fort Berthold Indian Agency.[47] The steamer returned to Fort Benton on July 24 with 350 tons of freight including sixty-two horses for the North-West Mounted Police at Fort Walsh.[48]

This particular arrival of the *Red Cloud* had significant impact on Fort

Table 6.9. Manifest of the steamboat *Red Cloud*
June 29, 1881, Bismarck to Fort Benton

I. G. Baker & Co., Fort Benton	3,436 packages
T. J. Todd & Co.	174 packages
George Steel, Sun River	84 packages
Spencer & Co., White Sulphur Springs	9 packages
T. W. Howard & Co.	15 packages
Lehman, Helena	283 packages
A. M. Holter & Bro., Helena	153 packages
J. R. Watson, Helena	244 packages
Conrad & H., Belmont	927 packages
J. L. Perkins	4 packages
Cochrane Ranch Co.	16 horses, 1 jack, 8 bulls, 2 dogs, 2 packages
T. C. Power & Bro.	1 car load lumber

Benton Weekly Record, June 30, 1881

Figure 6.7. North-West Mounted Police camp and post at Fort Walsh, 1878. National Archives of Canada, Ottawa (photograph no. C15281).

Benton. Mr. Starr, first mate and the Mounties favorite crewmember, was arrested and ultimately convicted for shooting and almost killing T. B. Cole, known as Tapioca, a local messenger for the Fort Benton hotel. When the *Red Cloud* landed, Tapioca jumped onto the gangplank of the docking vessel—creating a ruckus—and exchanged heated words with the first mate. The next morning in town at Brennan & Fisher's Saloon, a quarrel took place between the men, and Starr shot Tapioca, almost killing him.[49] It was for good reason that the *Red Cloud* left Fort Benton on July 25 without its popular first mate.

The *Red Cloud* was expected to return to Fort Benton one more time in 1881. Low water, however, plagued the operation of the boat in August and September. The boat was forced to unload its last cargo for the season downriver at Rocky Point. The stage of the river was so low, in fact, that the boat could not even make it to Fort Benton with an empty hold; this thwarted the *Red Cloud*'s hopes of being the first boat to ever attempt to winter at Fort Benton.[50]

Table 6.10. Manifest of the steamboat *Red Cloud* July 24, 1881, Bismarck to Fort Benton

I. G. Baker & Co., Fort Walsh	37 packages, 1 mare (this mare was carried all the way to Fort Benton)
Mounted Police, Fort Walsh	81 packages
Mounted Police, Fort McLeod	885 packages
Commissioner of Indian Affairs, Ft. McLeod	2 packages
Indian Department, Fort McLeod	18 packages
Hamilton & Hazlett, Old Agency	308 packages
Deposited at Coal Banks:	
I. G. Baker & Co., Fort Walsh	1,962 packages
Mounted Police, Fort Walsh	62 horses
C. Clark	1 package
A. M. Easter	1 package
A. W. Henry	1 package
W. T. Leavers	2 packages
Mrs. Downing	1 package
W. G. Conrad	1 package
M. Sullivan	1 package
T. Buchan	1 package
J. H. G. Bray	1 package
G. G. House	2 packages
W. D. Hyde	4 packages
Mrs. Conrad	3 packages
I. G. Baker & Co, Benton	1,073 packages

Benton Weekly Record, July 28, 1881

The amount of freight shipped up the Missouri River by all steamboat companies experienced a dramatic increase in 1881. In 1880, 10 million pounds of freight moved up the Missouri River; in 1881 the freight swelled to a remarkable 43 million pounds.[51] I. G. Baker & Company carried a significant part of that freight.

Despite having had the biggest freighting year recorded for Fort Benton and for I. G. Baker & Company, changes were at hand for Baker & Company at the end of the 1881 season. In October, the Baker firm sold its Fort Walsh store to its Fort Benton rival, T. C. Power & Brother and D. W. Marsh. In return, I. G. Baker & Company bought out T. C. Power's store and stock at Fort Macleod. Both firms agreed not to open competing interests in either location, and each thus secured a monopoly on the post trade.[52] I. G. Baker & Company had a good run at Fort Walsh. With the Indian and Mounted Police contracts, and any additional outside trade, the Fort Benton firm turned a handsome profit over the years. Charles Conrad commented that Baker & Company's decision to sell out to Power & Brother at Fort Walsh was based on the fact that the Canadians expected to abandon Fort Walsh for Fort Macleod (a fact that T. C. Power must not have known in advance of his purchase). Fort Macleod was located on an island, and there was concern that the entire post could be washed out. To preclude this possibility, it was anticipated that the post would be moved to a more favorable location 35 miles distant and new, more substantial and permanent buildings erected.[53] I. G. Baker & Company would move with them and keep the business the Fort generated.

7

Big Business on the Missouri River, 1882

> I recall as if it were yesterday, the crew standing on the lower deck and singing as we came into port, old southern favorites, such as "Suwanee River." There was the customary salute fired from the cannon on the levee and the "Red Cloud" whistled in reply, and all along the shore the people of the town come to bid the stranger welcome.
>
> —Lou Stocking Stewart, remembrance, 1937

Early in 1882, in advance of the opening of the Missouri River for the commercial season, Fort Benton's financial prospects looked bright. T. C. Power & Brother moved into its new dry goods store, and the firm-backed H. J. Wackerlin built a new brick hardware store next door. The Power firm even installed the first freight elevator in town—much to the fascination of both the locals and visitors. Miss Kitty Tongle gave up running the local ladies school to become the community's first female sales clerk. R. S. Culbertson got ready to lay the foundation for a new hotel, and John Houston opened Fort Benton's third brickyard. Once again I. G. Baker & Company won the Canadian North-West Mounted Police supply contracts, the beef contracts for the force, and the Indian annuities.

Warmed by the expectation of substantial profits, Baker & Company and T. C. Power & Brother agreed to a closer alliance. For 1882, they negotiated ways to maximize their control of river transportation. The two mercantile firms agreed to pool down freight rates on selected goods of other firms carried by their boats, and they agreed on the rate for carrying down their own goods.

They decided that whichever company's boat arrived in Fort Benton

Figure 7.1. The steamboat *Rosebud* (sometime after 1875), note the NWMP gathered along the shore. National Archives of Canada, Ottawa (photograph no. PA38690).

first would be the one to carry down all of the winter export freight collected by each company over the past winter's months. They further stipulated that the profit margin would be divided in proportion to the number of boats that each company fully owned in their fleet. Therefore, T. C. Power & Brother would receive four-fifths of the profit since they owned four boats and I. G. Baker & Company would have one-fifth of the profits for their single boat. Pooled freight rates from Benton to Bismarck applied to wool, robes, and pelts at $1 per 100 pounds; dry hides at 35 cents each; bailed calf hides $1 per 100 pounds; and bullion and ore at 35 cents per 100 pounds.[1] By pooling the freight rates and agreeing to send all of the down freight on the first boat to arrive in Benton, both firms guaranteed their hide and fur cargoes would hit the market at the seasonal high. The timing of I. G. Baker & Company's agreement with Power was important because it guaranteed that Baker's furs would be transported from Fort Benton to St. Louis before other hides flooded the market.

Another place for profit was the Canadian contracts to supply the various Indian agencies and Police posts in the Northwest Territory, which I. G. Baker and Company held for several years. The contract amounted to more than $450,000 to supply forage, provisions, and subsistence for twelve Indian agencies and the Mounted Police posts of Walsh, Macleod, Wood Mountains, Calgary, Qui'Appelle, Battleford, and Prince Albert's Mission.[2]

Besides the regular Northwest contracts, I. G. Baker & Company received a contract from the Canadian government to run a trimonthly mail service between Fort Macleod and Fort Benton during 1882.[3] Baker & Company's motivation was not for additional revenue in this case, rather the mail route resulted from a necessity for more regular correspondence between I. G. Baker & Company stores on both sides of the border. Seeking a way to improve the information exchange between posts without extra cost, I. G. Baker & Company convinced the Canadian government to fund a mail route. It was anticipated that the trimonthly mail route would be an improvement over the six- to eight-week variability of the previous years. Like most of I. G. Baker & Company's Canadian ventures, the firm maintained this contract for several years.[4]

In the spring of 1882, Baker & Company was awarded one more Canadian contract, this one to build a new Police post, Fort Calgary. I. G. Baker & Company's plans for building the post simultaneously caused an uproar within the Dominion Government and demonstrated the firm's forward thinking. Rather than build this fort out of wood like the previous Police posts, Baker & Company made known its desire that the Calgary fort should be built of brick, as would a new Company store at that location. The firm argued that "the erection of a substantial Police Post, would unquestionably be of material advantages . . . as Calgary is likely to become an important [location] in the N.W. Territory, the building of a good Police post is calculated to render [the] land (which might, hereafter be sold as a town site) much more valuable."[5]

As a result of the substantial increase in freighting expected in 1882, the Baker Line leased several boats for the season. The firm leased the *Key West* and the *Wyoming* from their independent owners[6] and the *General Terry* and *Nellie Peck* from the lower river Peck Line.[7] With the *Red Cloud*, these five boats carried a majority of the supplies up the Missouri River in 1882.[8] In fact, I. G. Baker & Company's leased boat, the *Key West*, carried down the first shipment of hides for Baker & Company and Power & Brother.[9] The flagship of the Baker Bonded Line, the *Red Cloud*, began the 1882 freighting season on March 15, when it left St. Louis for Fort Benton.[10]

The first arrival of the *Red Cloud* in 1882 was widely anticipated for the same reasons as previous years, but that season news had preceded the

Figure 7.2. Trading outfit outside of Fort Walsh, n.d.

steamer that the boat was scheduled to carry a hundred or so immigrants, known as the Patrick Colony, from Missouri.[11] The *Benton Weekly Record* reported that Isaac Baker wrote from St. Louis on March 21 saying that J. W. Patrick, a Fort Benton citizen, had organized a group of immigrants from Salem [Missouri], about 100 miles southeast of St. Louis, to come to Montana to settle as laborers. Baker added that he put about thirty of the immigrants on the *Red Cloud* when it left St. Louis and about sixty more were expected to board the vessel at Kansas City. Baker hoped that the ten or so families on their way to Fort Benton would be a good addition to the area's working class.[12] This is a distinct change from the gold hunters and fur trappers of the earlier days. Baker made the point that this group of im-

National Archives of Canada, Ottawa (photograph no. C19019B).

migrants was a "good class of American laborers." Baker further suggested that subsequent immigration would be encouraged if the merchants of Fort Benton could be persuaded to provide employment for those now traveling on the *Red Cloud.*

After many delays, the steamer arrived at Fort Benton on June 3,[13] after first dropping 205 Canadian Mounted Police at Coal Banks.[14] The boat brought in 450 tons of freight, and the whole community turned out to see the Patrick Colony. The colony included seventeen families and a few single men, all of whom traveled on the deck of the *Red Cloud.* Much to the dismay of Fort Benton's citizens, most of the Missouri immigrants arrived at Fort Benton rather impoverished. A local delegation took up a collection to help alleviate their needs, set up tents for temporary housing, and arranged jobs with several local businesses.[15]

The immigrants of the Patrick Colony were recruited by J. W. Patrick, a Fort Benton resident, for settlement in Barker, Montana. Many of the immigrants complained to the local newspaper upon arrival in Fort Benton that Mr. Patrick had cheated them into going to Montana. They told a variety of stories about how Patrick had purchased their farms for modest sums of money and paid the immigrants only portions of the total owed them before they boarded the *Red Cloud.* Most believed that Mr. Patrick would be waiting for them when they arrived in Fort Benton with the

Table 7.1. Manifest of the steamboat *Red Cloud*
June 7, 1882, St. Louis to Fort Benton

I. G. Baker & Co., Fort Benton	5,803 packages groceries
W. B. Settle, Benton	1 package
T. J. Todd & Co., Benton	9 packages
Dr. Parberry, White Sulphur Springs	78 packages merchandise
W. B. Edgar, Judith	6 packages
J. T. Lee, Sand Coulee	32 packages
W. B. Miller	5 packages
Charles Long	1 package
George Wolfe	4 boxes
J. R. Bright	19 packages
Mrs. Hendley	2 packages
D. G. Hagan	29 packages furniture
J. H. Rice	1 jersey cow
C. Long	1 coop chickens
Wm. Downs	15 bales robes

River Press, June 7, 1882; *Benton Weekly Record,* June 8, 1882

Table 7.2. Manifest of the steamboat *Red Cloud*
June 14, 1882, Fort Benton to Bismarck

I. G. Baker & Co., St. Louis	2,020 buffalo robes, 900 antelope skins, 950 deer skins, 170 elk skins, 150 mountain sheep skins, 10 bear skins, 1,000 muskrat skins, 500 badger skins, 100 skunk skins, 100 coyote skins, 400 beaver skins, 3,253 beef hides, 1 bale assorted furs
I. G. Baker & Co., Bismarck, D.T.	411 sacks potatoes, 400 empty beer cases

Benton Weekly Record, June 15, 1882

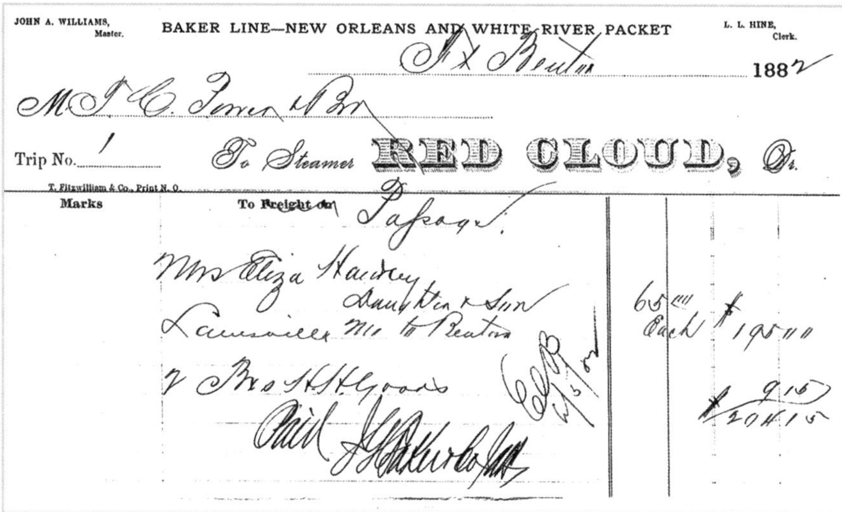
JOHN A. WILLIAMS, Master. BAKER LINE—NEW ORLEANS AND WHITE RIVER PACKET L. L. HINE, Clerk.

Ft Benton 1882

Trip No. 1 To Steamer RED CLOUD, Dr.

T. Fitzwilliam & Co., Print N. O.

Marks To Freight on Passage

Mrs Eliza Hardey daughter & Son Louisville Mo to Benton 65.00 Each $195.00

Figure 7.3. Passenger ticket receipt showing passage on the steamboat *Red Cloud* for Mrs. Eliza Hardey, daughter and son at $65 each. Montana Historical Society, Helena (Manuscript Collection 55(228-7)).

Table 7.3. Manifest of the steamboat *Red Cloud* June 25, 1882, Bismarck to Fort Benton

I. G. Baker & Co., Benton	5,201 packages
I. G. Baker & Co., Ft. Macleod	1,891 packages
I. G. Baker & Co., Calgary	132 packages
I. G. Baker & Co., Fort Walsh	23 packages
J. T. Todd & Co.	260 packages

Benton Weekly Record, June 29, 1882

remaining money owed them. Some of the immigrants received so little money from Patrick up front, in fact, that they had to beg Captain Williams of the *Red Cloud* for food while on the boat ride to Montana (deck passengers typically were responsible for feeding themselves). Several reported that they had heard that Patrick had sold their farms at auction for $600 after he had purchased the farms from the immigrants for only $100. Needless to say, Patrick's arrival back at Fort Benton was greatly anticipated. Despite their unfortunate experience, most of the immigrants eventually settled in Fort Benton.[16]

When the *Red Cloud* headed back downriver to Bismarck it carried what Benton newspapers estimated to be one of the largest cargoes of freight ever taken from Benton by a steamboat on one trip. In addition to the boat's usual variety of hides and furs the steamer carried down 411 sacks of potatoes and four hundred empty beer cases.

The steamer returned again to Fort Benton on June 25 with twelve more passengers for the Territory and another 400 tons of freight, consigned mainly to I. G. Baker & Company's establishments at Benton and the Canadian West.[17]

An estimated 14,000 tons of freight traveled up Montana's rivers in 1881. Between 1877 and 1882, the *Red Cloud* delivered more than 6,000 tons of freight to the Fort Benton levee and brought more than 3,000 passengers into Montana Territory. Given the number of contracts that I. G. Baker & Company won during 1882, the *Red Cloud* was a significant factor in the company's ability to fulfill its obligations. The June 25 arrival of the *Red Cloud,* however, was the last cargo the boat would ever deliver to the bustling river town of Fort Benton.

8

The Loss of the *Red Cloud* and the End of an Era: Fort Benton in Decline, 1882–85

> I feel the same way about it today as I did when I stepped ashore at Fort Benton fifty-seven years ago. My trip back from the states on the "Red Cloud" was the most pleasant of any journey I have ever made on a Missouri River steamboat.
>
> —Lou Stocking Stewart, remembrance, 1937

The Fort Benton *Record* told its readers that, for the first time since its establishment, it had to report the loss of a steamer. The *Red Cloud* struck a snag on July 11, 1882, about 200 miles below Fort Benton, and sank in three minutes. No lives were lost and the crew and passengers were transferred to the steamer *Rosebud,* which brought them to Fort Benton. Most of the hold cargo was lost as the vessel sank into the muddy bottom of the Missouri River.[1] The event was newsworthy for several reasons. Isaac G. Baker and several members of his family were onboard when the disaster happened, and the boat's captain at the time of the loss was John. A. Williams, a captain who already lost several steamboats during his career. Finally, and most alarmingly, the steamer was the flagship of a very successful local transportation line. For good reason, the local papers followed the accident with keen interest.

On July 12, Isaac Baker sent a telegram to the firm's Fort Benton office from Bouche's Grave. He stated that the boat was snagged and that the 3,000 bags of flour in the hold would be lost. He anticipated reshipping the passengers on the first available steamer.[2] T. J. Todd, captain of the *Big Horn,* the first steamer to arrive at the wreck site, sent a telegram the next day to Joseph Baker that his father and all of the passengers had been transferred to the *Rosebud.* He also noted that the deck freight was, in fact, saved, but that the hold freight was a total loss. More importantly, Todd mentioned that as the steamer sunk, it broke in two and that there was already water in the main cabin.[3] By July 19, the *River Press* further specified the wreck's location at just below Round Butte, downriver from the mouth of the Musselshell River.

A passenger's eyewitness account, printed in the local paper, gave Fort Benton's citizens the details of the steamboat's loss:

> The lower part of the bend [Bouche's Grave] is heavily timbered and very snaggy. The wind was blowing a blizzard from the northwest, but the steamer had passed the timber a[nd] escaped hitting the many snags and the captain was congratulating himself at having then passed all the difficult places in that one hundred miles section of the river, beginning at Spread Eagle and ending at Fort Peck, and lastly this snaggy bend at Bouche's Grave. The steamer had been proceeding up the bend under "slow belle," and five minutes before the accident Captain Williams, who was at the wheel, had just signaled the engineer to give her full head of steam when he saw the "break" of the snag, and he at once pulled the wheel hard down to starboard. It caught her larboard knuckle, about the forward hatchway, and from the crashing noise and the raised motion of her larboard guard and chimney it appeared to have torn her bottom from [the] foot of [the] cabin stairway to about midway of her boilers. The steamer's altered course in trying to avoid the snag sent her in about two lengths of the boat to within about two hundred feet of a middle bar, when she grounded in about five feet of water, and with about three feet of water in her hold, when she immediately filled with the entire larboard guard in the water.
>
> At first it was thought it would be necessary for safety to land the passengers on the sand bar with the yawl, but in less than half an hour the steamer *Big Horn* was seen about two miles away coming from above, but was soon lost to view behind a bend, but after waiting for an hour of anxious suspense it was evident she was wind-bound and the clerk and Mr.———, a passenger, was taken across the river where they could by walking a couple of miles reach the *Big Horn* and report our need of assistance. Captain Todd acted with promptness and worked his boat down opposite the wrecked *Red Cloud,* and was finally brought along side by means of a line being sent from the wreck to the *Big Horn* and with which she pulled herself over.

> The passengers were immediately transferred from the wreck with about forty tons of deck freight, which, the latter, was piled on the left-hand shore, and then another trip was made to the wreck bringing away some twenty tons more, of which there were two hundred sacks of flour reached by cutting open her deck on the "bar" or starboard side. At this time, 10 P.M., she had both careened and settled under the action of wind and current so that from her nosing to the after part of her boilers on the starboard side was the part above water.
>
> Arrangements were made with the steamer *Big Horn* to keep the passengers on board until she should meet an ascending boat. After she had proceeded about sixty miles the steamer *Rosebud* was met about 9 A.M. (twenty-four hours after the disaster) when the passengers were again transferred, and once more started for Montana's Metropolis, Fort Benton, and were landed several days afterwards.
>
> Captain Williams with a crew of men were left to secure and remove everything of value, but when the *Rosebud* passed up thirty-six hours after the sinking, the water had reached her cabin floor on the current or larboard side and it appeared likely she would soon capsize and break in pieces.[4]

I. G. Baker & Company did not successfully salvage the steamboat and her remaining cargo. The insurance underwriter paid off all claims, and the location of the wreck was subsequently called Red Cloud Bend and was labeled as such on several Missouri River survey maps following the loss.[5]

Despite I. G. Baker & Company's quarter of a million dollar profit in 1882, the sinking of the *Red Cloud* was a bad omen for the future for Baker & Company and the community of Fort Benton.[6] Ensuring continued freight movement and profits after the loss of the *Red Cloud,* Power & Brother's Block P Line and a few Coulson boats handled most of I. G. Baker & Company's river freighting needs for the rest of 1882 and for 1883.[7]

Although the loss of the *Red Cloud* was felt by the Fort Benton community, many expected the boom to continue with a repeat of 1882's profits. 1883, however, proved to be a hard season for many companies and their steamboats. On August 1, 1883, Power & Brother's (Block P) *Butte,* burned and was lost a few miles above old Fort Peck, Montana.[8] The old downriver company of Durfee and Peck no longer operated on the upper Missouri by 1883. In 1885, the Power Line's Block P bought the Coulson Line's last operating upper Missouri River boat, the *Rosebud.* With the sale, T. C. Power & Brother's Block P became the last steamboat line serving Fort Benton.[9]

In 1883, thirty-five boats came to Fort Benton, but by the end of the

1883 season Fort Benton was preparing for the impact of larger economic and transportation changes. It was not just steamboating that seemed so hard-hit in 1883. The whole of Fort Benton was in an irreversible slump. Only fifteen boats made it to the Fort Benton levee in 1884.[10] Numerous steamboat disasters in the preceding years were a presage of the changing times ahead. Financial adjustments of the early 1880s drastically altered the economic role of Fort Benton in the region. When the Canadian Pacific and Northern Pacific railways both bypassed Fort Benton in 1883 (Fort Benton was left in a 400-mile gap between the two lines), the once thriving steamboat hub slowly died of "commercial malnutrition."[11]

No longer was the Benton Road the Territory's most important highway—now the Northern Pacific's line to Helena held that title. The Canadian Pacific had the same effect on the shipments of goods into southwestern Alberta. Because the merchants in Helena knew the rail line would be completed soon, they held much of their 1883 freight requests until the lines were complete—the steamboats had noticeably less to carry that season. In August, the *Benton Weekly Record* reported that, "Benton streets look quiet."[12] Later the same paper suggested that "not even a dog fight relieved the monotony."[13]

Much like the Helena businesses, Fort Benton merchants were recognizing that times had changed again. Kleinschmidt & Brothers, one of Fort Benton's largest retail firms, decided to close its Fort Benton branch. Several others followed, including Gans & Klein and Davidson & Moffitt. One of the local saloons even felt the crunch of economic decline and advertised it would lower the cost of drinks to one bit (12.5 cents).[14] The big firms like I. G. Baker & Company and T. C. Power & Brother began scrambling to save some of their enterprise.

I. G. Baker & Company tried to counteract the loss of the *Red Cloud* and its Canadian enterprise via the Missouri River by making arrangements with Tees, Costigan, and Wilson, of Montreal, to ship its Canadian-purchased goods by steamer across the Great Lakes to Prince Arthur's Landing and then via the newly established Canadian Pacific Railway to their Northwest markets.[15] In July 1883, however, the last major bull train for Fort Macleod left Fort Benton, thus ending a 21-year commercial era.[16]

The 1885 Calgary business guide paid tribute to the era of I. G. Baker & Company's business enterprises when it noted that "in the balmy days of business done by this firm was something which may be measured by the word 'immense.' Their business principles have always squared with their actions, upon this line, as frontier traders, they built up a colossal trade, and made their business a financial success."[17] Years later William Conrad reflected that Fort Benton was an enterprise that had for its business activities "nearly a whole continent, that purchased goods from New Orleans on the south and the Great Slave Lakes on the north, almost within the Arctic circle and sold goods all over the world, in St. Louis and New York, in London and St. Petersburg, a business running into many millions of dollars."[18]

The sinking of the *Red Cloud* and the earlier loss of the *Colonel Macleod* marked the end of I. G. Baker & Company's interest in river steamboating. In 1885, Isaac G. Baker retired from active management of the business and William and Charles Conrad became the sole executives of I. G. Baker & Company. They, too, felt the pressure of a declining market and sinking economy. In the years following 1885, Baker & Company saw many of their Canadian contracts go to Canadian firms that utilized the finished Canadian rail system and undercut I. G. Baker & Company's freight rates. On September 3, 1890, the *Benton Weekly Record* gave notice that Gans & Klein were closing their doors and that I. G. Baker & Company were holding a close-out sale.[19]

In 1891, I. G. Baker & Company, as well as T. C. Power & Brother, sold their Canadian interests at Forts Macleod and Walsh to the Hudson's Bay Company. Years later, William Conrad recalled, upon Baker & Company's sale to the Hudson's Bay Company, the HBC manager drank a toast to the end of the firm that had "scaled down our stock from pounds to shillings."[20] That same year the Conrad brothers sold their holdings in I. G. Baker & Company to the Strain Brothers of Great Falls, Montana.[21] With the loss of its economic base and the subsequent departure of its founding merchants, Fort Benton passed from a bustling steamboat town into a sleepy rural Montana community.

A Full-Bellied River

The passing of the steamboat era at Fort Benton did not mean the end of steamboat history on the upper Missouri. The *Red Cloud,* for example, achieved renewed notoriety in the new century. On June 8, 1920, the *Helena Independent* reported from Eight Point, Montana, that Elmer Werner, a local man, had found the wreck of the *Red Cloud.* Werner stated that he discovered the wreck on May 29 close to a camp he established on the south side of the river nearly opposite Eight Point. He believed that the boat was approximately 20 feet below the surface in an island formed as a result of the river meandering around the wreck.[22] Werner attempted to salvage the wreck for any remaining cargo. After the brief news note, however, there is no additional mention of Werner's salvage attempt in local newspapers.[23]

In the 1930s, Franklin Roosevelt's New Deal came to the American West. It is estimated that the federal government spent more than $381 million in Montana. One of the most notable projects at the time was the construction of the Fort Peck Dam by the Works Progress Administration (WPA). The WPA began work on the Fort Peck Dam, the largest earth-

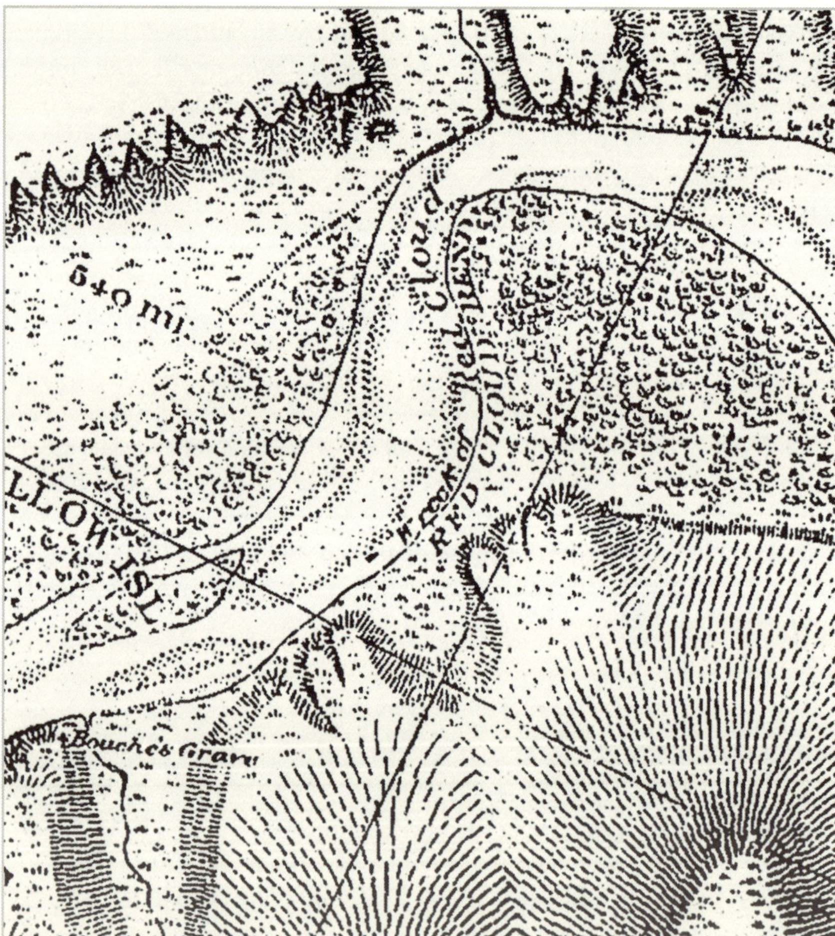

Figure 8.1. 1878 Missouri River Commission Survey map showing the location of the wreck of the *Red Cloud* and the bend known as Red Cloud Bend. Note the presence of Bouche's Grave, in the bottom left corner, given in newspaper accounts as the closest notable location to the wreck. National Archives, Washington D.C.

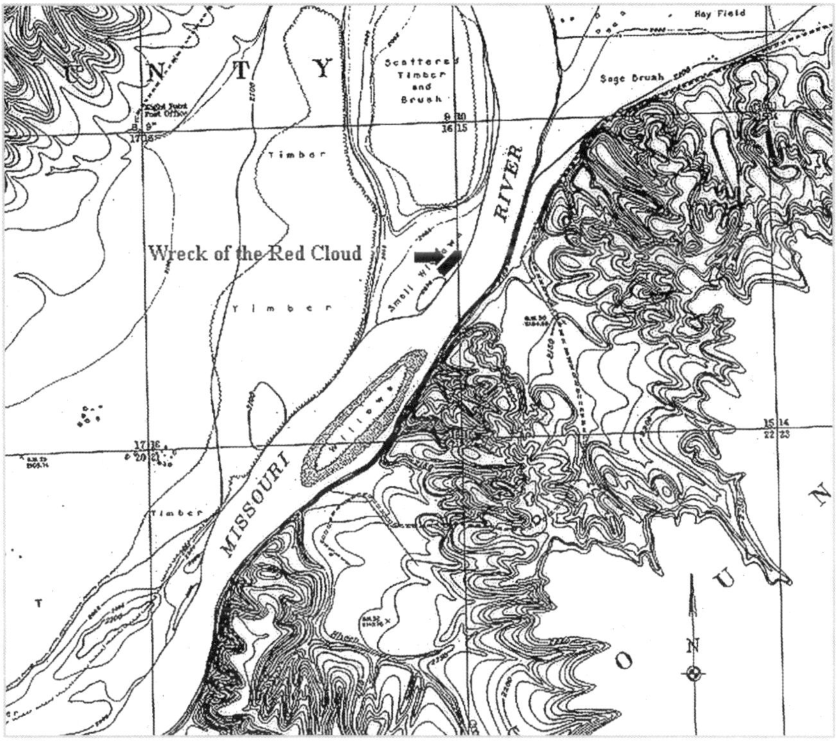

Figure 8.2. Location of the wreck of the *Red Cloud* superimposed on a map of the 1934 Fort Peck Reservoir Survey. U.S. Engineers Office, 1934, modified by the author.

filled dam in the world, in 1933. When completed, Fort Peck Dam stood 242 feet above the riverbed, was 9,000 feet across, and backed-up nearly 20 million acre feet of water.[24] This backed-up water protects the *Red Cloud* today.

The *Red Cloud* still lies in Red Cloud Bend of the 1880s Missouri River. Long before Elmer Werner believed that he had found the wreck of the *Red Cloud,* the Missouri River had shifted and left the wreck behind. The remains of the vessel and the bend that bore its name were absorbed into the surrounding landscape. Thus, when Werner claimed to have found the wreck, he was searching not in the river, but on an island that formed around the wreck and then became part of the riverbank.[25] The *Red Cloud* has not been in the Missouri River proper since about 1900. When the Fort Peck Dam was completed in 1937, the wreck of the *Red Cloud* was again inundated. Today the wreck lies deep beneath the bottom of the reservoir and more than 130 feet beneath the water's surface.

The *Red Cloud* is one of hundreds of vessels that were wrecked on the

Missouri River between 1819 and about 1920. For one hundred years, steamboats navigated the Missouri River, carrying supplies and people across the American West. Like the *Red Cloud,* each of those vessels has its own place in the story of the Missouri River West. Each carved out a niche within that history and each has the potential to retell its tale.[26]

The *Red Cloud,* like other steamers of its era, is an essential part of the history of the American West. Although much is written about the steamboat history of the American West, there is more to discover, especially the history that sank with the hundreds of steamboat wrecks and related sites on the upper Missouri River. The key to recovering one of the most tangible pieces of Missouri River steamboat history is to first tie that history to the individual communities that both depended on and fostered its growth. Dovetailing the *Red Cloud* to the "Life and Times" in which it operated, fully demonstrates its original importance. The *Red Cloud* was more than just a steamboat and certainly more than just a shipwreck; it was a piece of high commerce on the Great Plains, a symbol of wealth and new possibilities, a fortune gained and a fortune lost, a transporter of treasure never before seen, an exporter of natural resources, a favorite of the Canadian Mounted Police, and the embodiment of the most romanticized eras of American western history. Historically it remains a symbol of American ingenuity and the ideal of "Manifest Destiny."

Appendix A

"Up-River on the *Red Cloud*"

LOU STOCKING STEWART, 1937

May 27, 1880[1] is a date to be especially remembered by a number of Montana pioneers, myself among them, for it marked the arrival of the steamer "Red Cloud" at the Fort Benton levee after a continuous voyage of 77 days coming up the river from St. Louis. And I, personally, shall remember the day for still another reason, because it was my last trip on one of the early day steamboats.

The "Red Cloud," of the I. G. Baker line, was one [of] the largest boats on the river and one of the most palatial. A stern-wheeler, it measured 225 feet in length with a 34-foot beam. Upon this trip the boat was very heavily loaded with freight and carried some 200 passengers, the most of them bound for the port of Fort Benton. The long journey was partly due to this excess weight as the boat drew over four and one-half feet of water and was consequently hard to manage in the narrows and when negotiating rapids. Without its load aboard the boat had a drought of just over twenty inches.

As for the cargo, I might compare this trip of the "Red Cloud" to that of Noah's ark. We had aboard almost everything one could enumerate in the way of livestock—cattle, horses, mules, pigs, chickens, ducks and turkeys. Over my stateroom was chained a big Newfoundland dog that kept me awake nights by dragging his chain about. Then there was the usual tonnage of foodstuff, mainly salt pork, bacon and flour which was to be distributed at different towns along the river.

The passengers were a fine class of people, many of them on their first trip up river and determine[d] to make a success of western life. They were not adventurers, but homeseekers who later located throughout northern Montana. The more affluent occupied the upper deck cabins, while those who had yet to make a stake had more modest quarters on the lower or main deck. The two groups, while friendly, kept mostly to their own parts of the boat and each provided its own social diversions.

Captain McGarry was in charge of the "Red Cloud" and he and his officers were fine to everyone. We had three good meals each day, well cooked. The menu included bacon, beans, salt pork and all kinds of dried fruit, the latter a great luxury. Several times we had deer, antelope and buffalo meat for a change. The meals and service were just as regular as on an ocean liner.

As I have said, we traveled slowly on account of being so heavily loaded, then there were many stops to take on wood for the boilers. Almost every ten or fifteen miles along the upper river there were wood yards where cord wood was ricked up awaiting the boats. The steamers would put into shore and the wood would be carried aboard and corded up on the lower deck. In those days wood cutting was a paying business. The men would cut the wood and have it dried and ready for spring time, charging four or five dollars a cord. There was seldom a shortage, as timber of all kinds was plentiful along the Missouri river bottoms.

During the days when the weather was nice it was interesting to be out on deck for there was always something fascinating about watching the changing shore line, and who could ever forget the beauty of moonlight on the river! It was exciting to get the "feel" of the boat as it fought its way ahead in swift water with the paddle wheel churning a foamy ribbon in our wake, and to watch for the first glimpse of the unknown country around the bend just ahead. Then I liked to watch the deck hands as they sparred over a bar and the mate, stationed at the bow, continually sounding the channel for depth. In the lower reaches of the river we had little trouble, for the water was very high that year and had overflowed the lowlands. At St. Joe and Omaha it was nearly twenty miles wide.

Bottoms along the Missouri abounded with small game which we could often see plainly from the boat. We were many times in distance of buffalo which we usually sighted on the higher hills. However, one day a band of some 200 started to cross the river in front of the steamboat and we were compelled to lay up until they had passed across. The men tried to kill one, but the fur and hide were too thick for the shot to take effect. This was quite a novelty for the tenderfoot.

After leaving Sioux City, we saw Indians every day until we arrived at Fort Benton. They were trading skins, buffalo robes and other pelts at the different trading posts, Fort Randall, Fort Peck and Fort Berthold. When the boat landed, or tied up for the night, they would come aboard and take in the sights, and before leaving they would smoke their pipe of peace and then go. The old time river captains had very little trouble with the Indians as they were in the habit of being rather stern in their dealings and the braves knew that the privilege of coming aboard depended upon their good behavior. Their clothes were made of buckskin and they always wore gaudy blankets, with little colored beads, and shells in their hair. Faces were highly painted.

The finest lot of Indians we encountered was at Standing Rock, members of the Sioux tribe. I could not help but contrast this peaceable meeting with our stop at Standing Rock in June, 1876, when news of the Custer tragedy was brought in and twenty-four women, waiting there for news, learned that their husbands had been killed in the battle of the Big Horn.

One of the sights I saw at Fort Berthold on this trip was an Indian cemetery. They buried their dead upon poles, wrapped each brave in robes, with what he possessed such as guns, bows and arrows.

Two or three hundred miles before coming to Fort Benton the steamboats came through a rough country. The river was full of rapids and sandbars. The banks were high. Here we encountered many more delays due to the narrow channel and shallows. However, there were some striking rock formations along this part of the route. At Cannon Ball the rocks were shaped like a ball. At another point was a large rock, almost the size of a steamboat, which looked as though it had been carve[d] out by some person, but in reality it was nature's own work.

We rounded the butte and made fast at the Fort Benton levee on May 27th. Freight was unloaded, a new cargo put aboard and a few days later the "Red Cloud" was again headed down stream. She was wrecked a few years later on Wight Point, above Fort Peck, in what has ever since been known as Red Cloud Bend.

I shall never forget that eleven weeks on the Missouri River with its pleasant associations. There was dancing in the main cabin at night, with violins and guitars for the music (there was no piano aboard), square dances for the most part with the waltz another favorite. Then card games such as Pedro which was so popular at that time. I recall as if it were yesterday the crew standing on the lower deck and singing as we came into port, old southern favorites such as "Suwanee River." There was the customary salute fired from the cannon on the levee and the "Red Cloud" whistled in reply, and all along the shore the people of the town come to bid the stranger welcome.

I feel the same way about it today as I did when I stepped ashore at Fort Benton fifty-seven years ago. My trip back from the states on the "Red Cloud" was the most pleasant of any journey I have ever made on a Missouri river steamboat.[2]

Appendix B

"To P. S. Starr"

CANADIAN NORTH-WEST MOUNTED POLICE, 1881

To P. S. Starr, Eq., the bright luminary who has shed his beneficent effulgence over the benighted sons of Canada who have "gamboled" as innocent lambs in the glorious sunshine, and also in the umbrageous shade of the rubicund nebulosity (*alias Red Cloud*).

The desideratum of our hearts will ever be that you may live to the age of Methuselah and never die till you do so, in the middle of a thousand-acre prairie where you will have room to make a grand final kick. May you ever shine as a luminous *Starr*, undimmed, and never condescend to "shoot" or commit any other meteorological idiosyncrasy, and that you may never have to partake of the benefits of an eleemosynary institution.

We can not close this, our little address, without paying a tribute of eulogy and thanksgiving for the innumerable times you have entertained us with your graphic, loquacious and ever truthful descriptions of the delighted scenery and events that have occurred from time to time, and which in you we have found a source of unprecedented information for all our inquiries.

Twinkle, twinkle little Star(r),
How we'll wonder where you are;
When from you we're far away
We'll oftimes pause and say,
How's our little Starr to-day;
Is he well or is he ailing—
Is he on the "Red Cloud" sailing?
Is he swearing at "them niggers?"
In which trait he often figures,
Promising jobs to grave-yard diggers.[1]

Notes

INTRODUCTION

1. May Flanagan was the niece of T. C. Power, I. G. Baker's sometimes chief rival and sometimes best business partner. She grew up around the old garrison fort of Fort Benton. Flanagan, "A Perspective on the Life and Times of I. G. Baker [1940s]," May G. Flanagan Papers, Small Collection 1236, Montana Historical Society, Helena (hereafter MHS).

2. Flanagan, "A Perspective," MHS.

3. Corbin, "Steamboat Archaeology on the Missouri River," 316.

4. *Benton Weekly Record*, July 20, 1882.

CHAPTER 1

1. O'Sullivan, "The Nation of Futurity," *Democratic Review* 6 (1839): 427; O'Sullivan, "Territorial Aggrandizement," *Democratic Review* 17 (1845): 243–48; Pratt, "John O'Sullivan and Manifest Destiny," *New York History* 14 (1933): 221; Weinberg, *Manifest Destiny*, 107, 111–12, 144–45; Merk, *Manifest Destiny and Mission in American History*, 24.

2. Pratt, "John O'Sullivan and Manifest Destiny," 222–23.

3. Father Marquette was a French Jesuit priest stationed at a mission not far from present-day Duluth, Minnesota, during the 1670s. His companion, Joliet, was a local trader. In 1673 Marquette wrote to his superiors about his discovery of the Mississippi and then subsequently the Missouri River. Sheldon, "Discovery and Exploration," *Nebraska History* 8, no. 1 (1927): 5.

4. Father Marquette's discovery of the Missouri River, in Sheldon, "Discovery and Exploration," 5.

5. Corbin, *Material Culture of Steamboat Passengers*, i.

6. Chittenden, *American Fur Trade of the Far West*, 35.

7. Ibid.

8. Ibid.

9. Flanagan, "A Perspective," MHS; Murphy, *Half Interest in a Silver Dollar*, 12; Harber, *Our Fort Benton*, 15.

10. Flanagan, "A Perspective," MHS.

CHAPTER 2

1. Chittenden argues that this post was established well up the Missouri River as an early trading post and as a solid presence in Spanish territory. Chittenden, *American Fur Trade of the Far West*, 75, 947; Swagerty, "Indian Trade in the Trans-Mississippi West to 1870," 356–60; Norall, *Bourgmont, the Explorer of the Missouri*, 46–47.

2. Oglesby, *Manuel Lisa and the Opening of the Missouri Fur Trade*, 54.

3. Schwantes, *Long Day's Journey*, 53.

4. Vestal, *The Missouri*, 15–16.

5. Keelboats averaged between 7 and 10 feet in beam and drew no more than 2 feet

of water fully loaded. Often the boats had a cabin or cargo box in the middle with a clearance of about 6 feet where the cargo was stored and where passengers could find shelter. A 12- to 18-inch-wide cleated footway ran along both gunwales where the crew walked while poling the boat. Often there were four to twelve rowers in the bow who sometimes gained assistance from a square sail, although many keelboats did not bother to even carry their sails because of the unpredictability of the wind. The boat was steered by means of a long oar pivoted at the stern. Baldwin, *Keelboat Age on Western Waters,* 39–55; Schwantes, *Long Day's Journey,* 53–54; Vestal, *The Missouri,* 16.

6. Schwantes, *Long Day's Journey,* 48.

7. Vestal, *The Missouri,* 51.

8. Fitch, "The Missouri, Its Habits and Eccentricities Described by a Personal Friend," *American Magazine* 63, no. 6 (1907): 640; Vestal, *The Missouri,* 52.

9. Fitch, "The Missouri," 640.

10. *Missouri Intelligencer,* May 28, 1819; Vestal, *The Missouri,* 53.

11. *St. Louis Enquirer,* June 9, 1819; Peterson, "Log of the *Henry M. Shreve* to Fort Benton," *Mississippi Historical Review* 31 (1945): 538; McBride, "Steamboating on the Upper Missouri," 2; Hunter, *Steamboats on Western Rivers,* 47; Winther, *Transportation Frontier, Trans-Mississippi West,* 78; Lass, *History of Steamboating on the Upper Missouri River,* 6; Corbin, "Shifting Sand and Muddy Water: Historic Cartography and River Migration as Factors in Locating Steamboat Wrecks on the Far Upper Missouri River," *Historical Archaeology* 32, no. 4 (1998): 86.

12. Lass, *History of Steamboating on the Upper Missouri River,* 5–8.

13. *Missouri Gazette & Public Advertiser,* July 10, 1818, and May 26, 1819; McBride, "Steamboating," 6; Lass, *History of Steamboating on the Upper Missouri River,* 6; Havighurst, "Steamboat to the Rockies," *American West* 7, no. 5 (1970): 5.

14. The *Western Engineer* was built specifically for Long's expedition and had a unique construction. The vessel was a small stern-wheeler, 75 feet x 13 feet, that drew only 19 inches light. The bow was painted to imitate a large serpent that also blew smoke (steam) out its mouth. It had a notable impact on the native inhabitants. The *Western Engineer* was wintered 5 miles below old Council Bluffs, thus becoming the first steamboat to ever winter on the Missouri. Jones, "Steamboating on the Nebraska Shore," *Nebraska History* 8, no. 1 (1925): 12; Peterson, "Log of the *Henry M. Shreve* to Fort Benton," 537; McBride, "Steamboating," 14; Jackson, *Voyages of the Steamboat* Yellow Stone, 20; Schwantes, *Long Day's Journey,* 50.

15. Corbin, *Material Culture,* 3.

16. Chappell, "River Navigation," *Transactions of the Kansas State Historical Society 1905–1906* 9 (1906): 73; McBride, "Steamboating," 27; Lass, *History of Steamboating on the Upper Missouri River,* 8.

17. The *Yellow Stone* was built in Louisville, Kentucky, in 1830. It was a side-wheel, single engine vessel, 130 feet x 19 feet, with a 6 foot mean depth of hold. The steamer had cabins in the stern hold, open boiler decks, no hurricane roof and an elevated pilot house. The boat drew 6 feet fully loaded at a maximum of 75 tons. Chappell, "River Navigation," 280; Jackson, *Yellow Stone,* 159–66; McBride, "Steamboating," 40.

18. When the *Yellow Stone* left Fort Tecumseh for St. Louis on July 15, it carried down a large cargo of buffalo robes, furs, peltries, and 10,000 pounds of buffalo tongues. *Missouri Intelligencer,* August 6, 1831; Chittenden, *American Fur Trade of the Far West,* vol. 1, 339; McBride, "Steamboating," 41.

19. Peterson, "Log of the *Henry M. Shreve* to Fort Benton," 537; Hunter, *Steamboats on Western Rivers,* 48; Winther, *Transportation Frontier,* 80; Jackson, *Steamboat* Yellow Stone, 2; Cassler, *Steamboats of the Fort Union Fur Trade,* 2; Corbin, *Material Culture,* 3–4.

20. The *Assiniboine* was built in Cincinnati, Ohio, in 1833 for the American Fur Company. It was a side-wheel steamer, 130 feet x 20 feet x 6 feet. The boat spent the winter of 1834 stranded near Fort Union due to low water. The boat managed to return downriver in the spring of 1835, only to catch fire and burn near the mouth of the Cannon Ball River on June 1, 1835. Cassler, *Steamboats of the Fort Union Fur Trade,* 19.

21. McBride, "Steamboating," 51.

22. Schwantes, *Long Day's Journey,* 48.

23. Lass, *History of Steamboating on the Upper Missouri River,* 11.

24. The *Robert Campbell* was a side-wheel packet built in Hannibal, Missouri, in 1849. The boat was rated at 268 tons and was burned and lost in a wharf fire at St. Louis on October 13, 1853. Way, *Way's Packet Directory,* 395.

25. Lass, "Missouri River Steamboating," *North Dakota History* 56, no. 3 (1989): 3.

26. Winther, "Early Commercial Importance of the Mullan Road," *Oregon Historical Quarterly* 46, no. 1 (1945): 22.

27. Mullan, "Report on the Construction of a Military Road from Fort Walla-Walla to Fort Benton," *Senate Documents,* 37 Cong., 2 sess., Doc. 43, 5; Winther, "Early Commercial Importance," 23; T. C. Elliot, "The Mullan Road: Its Local History and Significance," *Washington Historical Quarterly* 14, no. 3 (1923): 207.

28. Winther, "Early Commercial Importance," 23–26.

29. Ibid., 28; Howard, "Captain John Mullan," *Washington Historical Quarterly* 25, no. 3 (1934): 193; Malone, Roeder, and Lang, *Montana,* 73.

30. Malone, Roeder, and Lang, *Montana,* 72.

31. Lass, "Missouri River Steamboating," 3–4.

32. Raynolds, "Report on the Exploration of the Yellowstone River," *Annual Report of the Chief of Engineers,* 4; Lass, *History of Steamboating on the Upper Missouri River,* 15.

33. Lass, *History of Steamboating on the Upper Missouri River,* 13–15.

34. Ibid., 14–15.

35. Between 1833 and 1859, boats of the American Fur Company pushed farther upriver each season. In 1834 the *Assiniboine* journeyed 100 miles above the mouth of the Yellowstone River, near the mouth of Poplar River, and had to winter there on account of low water. In 1853 the *El Paso* reached a point 125 miles farther yet, a few miles below the mouth of the Milk River. Chittenden, *History of Early Steamboat Navigation on the Missouri River,* 36–37; McBride, "Steamboating," 53; Havighurst, "Steamboat to the Rockies," 9.

36. The *Chippewa* was a stern-wheel packet built in Belle Vernon, Pennsylvania, in 1857. The boat was 160 feet x 30 feet and rated at 173 tons. The boat operated on the Upper Mississippi in the Northwestern Line from 1858 through 1859 when it transferred to the Missouri River. Way, *Way's Packet Directory,* 86.

37. The *Spread Eagle* was a side-wheel packet built in Brownsville, Pennsylvania, in 1857. The boat was 210 feet x 36 feet x 6 feet and rated at 389 tons. The boat spent its career operating on the Missouri River. Way, *Way's Packet Directory,* 431.

38. *The Nebraskian,* June 11, 1859, and August 20, 1859; Chouteau, "Report of Chas. P. Chouteau to Secretary of War of a Steamboat Expedition from St. Louis to Fort Benton, 1859," *Contributions to the Historical Society of Montana* 3 (1859): 255; Hunter, *Steamboats on Western Rivers,* 49; Lass, *History of Steamboating on the Upper Missouri River,* 15–19.

39. The *Key West* was a stern-wheel packet built in Elizabeth, Pennsylvania, in 1857. The boat was rated at 169 tons. Way, *Way's Packet Directory,* 271.

40. Michael A. Leeson, ed., *History of Montana, 1739–1885,* p. 393.

41. Chittenden, *History of Early Steamboat Navigation on the Missouri River,* 218; Lass, *History of Steamboating on the Upper Missouri River,* 15–19; Overholser, *Fort Benton,* 33; Corbin, "Shifting Sand and Muddy Water," 86.

42. Winther, "Early Commercial Importance," 28.

43. Ibid., 29–30; see also Stuart, *Forty Years on the Frontier,* and Bancroft, *History of Washington, Idaho, and Montana.*

44. Oviatt, "Pacific Coast Competition," *Pacific Northwest Quarterly* 56, no. 4 (1965): 168; Winther, "Early Commercial Importance," 29–30.

45. Oviatt, "Pacific Coast Competition," 168; Winther, "Early Commercial Importance," 30; Albright, "The Relations of Montana with the Federal Government," 40; Bancroft, *History of Washington,* 629.

46. Madsen, "The Montana Trail: Salt Lake City–Corinne to Fort Benton," *Overland Journal* 13, no. 1 (1995): 19–22; Havighurst, "Steamboat to the Rockies," 10.

47. Oviatt, "Pacific Coast Competition," 168–69.

48. Ibid., 170.

49. Chittenden, "Ancient Town of Fort Benton," *Magazine of Western History* (December 1890): 422; Wood, "Fort Benton's Part in the Development of the West," *Washington Historical Quarterly* 10, no. 3 (1929): 218; Winther, "Early Commercial Importance," 31.

50. Parsons, "Steamboats in the 'Idaho' Gold Rush," *Montana: The Magazine of Western History* 10, no. 1 (1960): 53–54; Lass, "Missouri River Steamboating," 5.

51. Lass, "Missouri River Steamboating," 5.

52. Overholser, "Big Muddy Builds Montana," in *Our Fort Benton,* 24.

53. William M. Wheatley to John Wheatley, letter dated March 18, 1866, from Gravis Mills, Missouri. Robert W. Binkley Collection, London, Ontario.

54. William continues with information that the man never actually kept his hard-worked fortune because he would often go into Helena and Virginia City where he would spend a $1,000 a day drinking and gambling. Robert W. Binkley Collection.

55. Chittenden, *History of Early Steamboat Navigation on the Missouri River,* 237–39; Peterson, "Log of the *Henry M. Shreve* to Fort Benton," 538; Lass, *History of Steamboating on the Upper Missouri River,* 21; Petsche, *Steamboat* Bertrand, 117; Corbin, *Material Culture,* 4–5.

56. Overholser, *Fort Benton,* 59–60.

57. Steamboat profits in the mountain trade in 1866 were quite large; the *Cora* made $50,000 on one trip, the *Deer Lodge* $45,000; salt was bought at $1.45 a barrel in St. Louis and sold for $45 a barrel at the Montana mines. Overholser, "The Big Muddy," 24; Overholser, *Fort Benton,* 60–61.

58. Malone, Roeder, and Lang, *Montana,* 73.

59. *Montana Post,* September 29, 1866.

60. *Montana Post,* July 24, 1868; Oviatt, "Pacific Coast Competition," p. 175.

61. Lass, "Missouri River Steamboating," 6; Lass, *From the Missouri River to the Great Salt Lake,* 131–32.

62. Winther, "Early Commercial Importance," 34.

63. Sharp, "Whoop-Up Trail," *Pacific Historical Review* 21 (1952): 130.

64. Overholser, "The Big Muddy," 24.

CHAPTER 3

1. In 1850, Baker married Ann Isabelle Dawes, of Diamond City, Montana Territory. Four years after her death, in 1858, he married Frances Wilson of Lexington, Missouri. Flanagan, "A Perspective," MHS; *St. Louis Globe Democrat,* April 6, 1904.

2. Little is known about Josiah Smart. Pierre Chouteau Jr. was long involved with the history of the upper Missouri fur trade era. Initially, the three traded at the Osage River Agency supplying the Sac and Fox Indians. In July of 1848, Chouteau pulled out of the partnership, selling his third back to Baker and Smart. By November of the same year, Baker and Smart dissolved their partnership as well, since the two were at odds over the appropriate management of several trade houses in the region. One finds a hint of the difficulty in a letter to John B. Sarpy, dated January 1850. Baker lamented, "you stated that the Sac and Fox locations were suitable for me. By embarking on that trade I could remove the odium that is now hanging over me. It might be well not to mention this to Smart as he thinks himself capable of carrying on both houses." There is no distinct explanation regarding why Baker and Smart severed their partnership. It is clear, however, that by 1855, Baker had another partner, Alexander Street. Baker and Street operated a general freighting business out of St. Louis for several years. For a discussion of his involvement and the general history of the fur trade see Chittenden, *American Fur Trade of the Far West,* and Phillips, *The Fur Trade,* 389–429.

3. From 1864 through 1867 Baker had trade and financial affiliations with Chouteau, either as an agent for the Benton post, or, after the separation, for debts still owed Baker. "Letters," Chouteau-Papin Collection, Missouri Historical Society Archives, St. Louis, Missouri; Flanagan, "A Perspective," MHS.

4. Murphy, *Half Interest in a Silver Dollar,* 17.

5. Flanagan, "A Perspective," MHS.

6. Sharp, *Whoop-Up Country,* 213; Murphy, *Half Interest in a Silver Dollar,* 19.

7. Murphy, *Half Interest in a Silver Dollar,* 20.

8. Ibid., 22.

9. Ibid.

10. Sanders, *History of Montana,* 994–96; Stout, *Montana,* 1030–31.

11. Charles E. Conrad Papers, Small Collection 340, Montana Historical Society, Helena; Anonymous, *History of Montana,* 1009; Miller, *Illustrated History of the State of Montana,* 510–11; Anonymous, *Progressive Men of the State of Montana,* 903–905.

12. For a discussion of the roles of the Conrad brothers in I. G. Baker & Company and the development of business in Montana see Halvorson, "Charles E. Conrad of Kalispell," *Montana: The Magazine of Western History* 21, no. 2 (1971): 56–67; Klassen, "I. G. Baker and Company in Calgary," *Montana: The Magazine of Western History* 35, no. 3 (1985): 40–55; Sharp, "Merchant Princes of the Plains," *Montana: The Magazine of Western History* 5, no. 1 (1955): 2–20.

13. Many scholars (Sharp, Klassen, Murphy, and others) suggest that once Isaac Baker left Fort Benton and after George Baker sold his shares to the Conrad brothers, both basically dropped out of the Fort Benton enterprise. This is incorrect. Isaac Baker never relinquished his hold on his company and he certainly never took a back seat to the Conrads as others have suggested.

14. Sharp, "Merchant Princes of the Plains," 10–15; *The Bearpaw Mountaineer* (Montana Territory), "Merchant Princes of Pioneer Times; How one house served North-

west," undated news article found in the Vertical Files of the Montana Historical Society, Helena.

15. Lass, "Steamboating on the Missouri," *Journal of the West* 7, no. 1 (1967): 57–58.

16. Hammer, "River and Rail," *Journal of the West* 17, no. 4 (1978): 43–44; Lass, "Missouri River Steamboating," 6, and "Steamboating on the Missouri," 60.

17. Oviatt, "Fort Benton, River Capital," 150; Lass, "Missouri River Steamboating," p. 5; Robert M. Utley, "The Dash to Promontory," *Utah Historical Quarterly* 29, no. 2 (1961): 98.

18. *Benton Weekly Record,* June 1, 1875; Oviatt, "Fort Benton, River Capital," 150.

19. *New Northwest* [Deer Lodge], December 24, 1869.

20. Malone, Roeder, and Lang, *Montana,* 75.

21. Madsen and Madsen, "The Diamond R Rolls Out," *Montana: The Magazine of Western History* 21, no. 2 (1971): 3.

22. *Montana Post,* April 16, 1869.

23. Madsen and Madsen, "The Diamond R Rolls Out," 4.

24. Ibid., 6, 14.

25. Oviatt, "Fort Benton, River Capital," 150–51.

26. The Whoop-Up trail ran from the head of steamboat navigation at Fort Benton on the Missouri River to Fort MacLeod on the Oldman. This route was the principal way in which goods reached the Canadian western plains until the building of the Canadian Pacific railroad in 1883. See Sharp, *Whoop-Up Country.*

27. Oviatt, "Fort Benton, River Capital," 150–51.

28. Ibid., 151.

29. Sharp, "Whoop-Up Trail," 133–43; Oviatt, "Fort Benton, River Capital," 151.

30. Sharp, "Whoop-Up Trail," 133–35.

31. Murphy, *Half Interest in a Silver Dollar,* 33; Breen, *Canadian Prairie West and the Ranching Frontier,* 7.

32. Murphy, *Half Interest in a Silver Dollar,* 33.

33. For a full discussion of the Fenian Invasion of 1866, see Rodgers, *Guardian of the Great Lakes,* 78–93, 106–20.

34. Sharp, *Whoop-Up Country,* 55.

35. For the best overview of the Cypress Hills Massacre see Sharp, *Whoop-Up Country,* chapter 4. Scholars supporting the Cypress Hills Massacre as the impetus for the NWMP include: Denny, *Law Marches West,* Berry, *Whoop-Up Trail,* and Sharp. For a detailed explanation of the original plan for establishing the NWMP by Captain C. F. Butler see Macleod, "The North-West Mounted Police 1873–1905," chapter 2.

36. Macleod, *North-West Mounted Police,* 3.

37. Ibid., 3–4.

38. Ibid., 4–5.

39. Ibid., 7–8; see also Gluek, *Minnesota and the Manifest Destiny of the Canadian Northwest.*

40. Macdonald Papers, vol. 518, Macdonald to Cartier, June 16, 1871, National Archives of Canada, Ottawa; Macleod, *North-West Mounted Police,* 8–11.

41. Macdonald Papers, vol. 252, Morris to Macdonald, November 16, 1872, and January 17, 1873, National Archives of Canada, Ottawa; Macleod, *North-West Mounted Police,* 12–14.

42. Robertson-Ross was the second survey and report of the Canadian northwest after the Dominion acquisition of the HBC land. The first survey was conducted in 1870 by Captain W. F. Butler who, in his report, warned of the inevitable shock and resulting trouble concerning encroachment on natives' lands. In his 1871 report Butler recommended the formation of a police force of one hundred to 150 men, one-third to be mounted, to help ease the transition. Butler, *The Great Lone Land,* 357–80; Macleod, *North-West Mounted Police,* 14–15.

43. Alexander Campbell Papers, S. L. Tilley to Campbell, December 3, 1872, National Archives of Canada, Ottawa.

44. Macleod, *North-West Mounted Police,* 15.

45. Macleod, "The North-West Mounted Police," 36–38; Horrall, "Sir John A. Macdonald and the Mounted Police Force for the Northwest Territories," *Canadian Historical Review* 53(1972): 197; Francis, "Business, Enterprise, and the National Policy," 15. Also see Francis, "Montana Business and Canadian Regionalism in the 1870s and 1880s," *Western Historical Quarterly* 12, no. 3 (1981): 291–304.

46. Sharp, *Whoop-Up Country,* 81.

47. See Macleod, "Northwest Mounted Police," chapter 3, for the most descriptive depiction of the Long March.

48. French, "Report of the Commissioner, North-West Mounted Police, 1874," 50.

49. Overholser, *Fort Benton,* 360.

50. Shirley Carter Ashby Diary, 1916, Small Collection 283, MHS; Overholser, *Fort Benton,* 360.

51. William Conrad responded to the Canadian government on May 9, 1873, providing rates for Canadian hauls from various points on the Canadian Pacific Railway. Murphy, *Half Interest in a Silver Dollar,* 24.

52. Shirley Carter Ashby Diary, 1916, Small Collection 283, MHS.

53. For information concerning Dewdney's varied roles in the Canadian West see Sharp, *Whoop-Up Country.*

54. Ibid., 221–22.

55. Denny was an inspector for the NWMP and served for eight years. He was well acquainted with the Montana firms and their influence in the Canadian West. Denny, *Law Marches West,* 39; Overholser, *Fort Benton,* 360; Murphy, *Half Interest in a Silver Dollar,* 35–36.

56. RG 18, series A-1, vol. 4, file 98-75, "Statement of Mr. I. G. Baker, Fort Benton, Montana, 25 February 1875," National Archives of Canada, Ottawa; Sharp, *Whoop-Up Country,* 87.

57. Sharp, *Whoop-Up Country,* 82.

58. Ibid., 88–89; Overholser, *Fort Benton,* 360; Murphy, *Half Interest in a Silver Dollar,* 37.

59. denOtter, "Hudson's Bay Company's Prairie Transportation Problem," 35.

60. *Herald* (Helena, Montana Territory), October 9, 1874.

61. Sharp argues that Fort Whoop-Up was the most famous of the old whiskey forts. It was located at the junction of the St. Mary and Oldman rivers and quickly became the primary center in the Indian trade between Fort Benton and Fort Edmonton. The fort was originally built by John Healy and A. B. Hamilton (nephew of Isaac G. Baker) in 1869. Sharp, *Whoop-Up Country,* 48.

62. I. G. Baker & Company built Fort Calgary in 1875; the fort consisted of a main

stockade with a collection of log buildings about a quarter mile from the main post that served as Baker & Company's trading store and Calgary headquarters. Burns & Eliot Co., *Calgary, Her Industry and Resources,* 16.

63. Elizabeth Beaty was the daughter of the managing editor of the Toronto *Leader.* Nevitt wrote to her almost every day during the winter of 1874–75. Richard Barrington Nevitt was a refugee of the U.S. Civil War who sought shelter in Canada and never returned to the states. Nevitt served as assistant surgeon of the NWMP, spending the winter of 1874–75 at Fort Macleod with Denny. Nevitt, *A Winter at Fort Macleod,* 8.

64. Ibid., 92–93.

65. C. T. Bridges, "Statement," Extracts from Hudson's Bay Company Records, Peigan Post, 1833–83, Glenbow-Alberta Institute, Calgary; Francis, "Business, Enterprise, and National Policy," 23. For the most complete telling of I. G. Baker & Company's Calgary enterprise see Klassen, "I. G. Baker & Co. in Calgary," *Montana: The Magazine of Western History* 35, no. 3 (1985): 42–55.

66. By the end of the first winter T. C. Power & Brother would also build a trading store at Fort Macleod. On March 10, 1875, Baker & Company delivered a large number of fresh horses from the Sun River country for the Mounties. Denny, *Law Marches West,* 61, 84–85; Nevitt, *A Winter at Fort Macleod,* 70; Overholser, *Fort Benton,* 360; Murphy, *Half Interest in a Silver Dollar,* 38.

67. Denny, *Law Marches West,* 60; Nevitt, *A Winter at Fort Macleod,* 30.

68. Overholser, *Fort Benton,* 85, 363.

69. *Herald,* October 14, 1874.

70. The *Benton* was a stern-wheel packet built in Pittsburgh in 1874–75. The boat was 197 feet x 33 feet. x 5 feet; the steamer drew a mere 18 inches light. The boat departed Pittsburgh on its maiden voyage with Captain James McGarry, master, and Joseph S. Hill as clerk. The *Benton* arrived at Fort Benton for the first time on May 27, 1875, thus commencing a long career on the Missouri River. The steamer made forty-four trips to Fort Benton during its career, more than any other boat in the history of the Missouri River mountain trade. "Bill of Sale," file 13A-10, Thomas C. Power Papers, Manuscript Collection 55, MHS; Way, *Way's Packet Directory,* 50.

71. Oviatt, "Fort Benton, River Capital," 151.

72. Isaac's brother, George A. Baker, remained heavily involved in the St. Louis business. After selling his shares in the Fort Benton trade to the Conrads, he acted as agent and co-owner of the steamboat business with Isaac through the Olive Street office. *Bismarck Semi-Weekly Tribune,* June 26 and July 24, 1875; April 11, 1877. The *C. W. Mead* (General Mead) was a stern-wheel packet built in 1875 in Pittsburgh; it was owned and operated by the Kountz Line; the *Fontenelle* was a stern-wheel packet built in 1870 in Brownsville, Pennsylvania, for Captain John H. Shaw and was often leased to companies operating on the Missouri River; Way, *Ways Packet Directory,* 169, 182.

73. *St. Louis Democrat,* as reprinted in the *Benton Weekly Record,* May 1, 1875.

74. Baker & Company's Fort Benton post shipped down 19,280 buffalo robes, 650 calf robes, 25 tons of antelope, deer and elk skins, 503 wolf skins, 1,700 fox skins, 33 bear skins, and 1,300 pounds of beaver skins. *Benton Weekly Record,* August 1, 1875.

75. Nevitt, *A Winter at Fort Macleod,* 120.

76. The *Josephine* was a stern-wheel packet 183 feet x 31 feet that drew less than 4 feet. The boat was built on the orders of Joseph LaBarge to be run by Captain Grant Marsh

as part of the U.S. military fleet. See Gamble, "Up River to Benton," *Montana: The Magazine of Western History* 6, no. 2 (1956): 40–41.

77. *Benton Weekly Record,* June 22 and July 31, 1875.

78. *Benton Weekly Record,* May 5, 1876.

79. *Benton Weekly Record,* May 19, 1876.

80. RG 18, series A-1, vol. 11, file 248-76, "Baker & Co. to Canadian Secretary of State Richardson — June 7, 1876," National Archives of Canada, Ottawa.

81. RG 18, series A-1, vol. 9, file 92-76, "Baker & Co. — 1876"; vol. 10, file 170-76, "Contract for supply of pay from Baker & Co. 1876–77"; vol. 11, file 248-76, "Baker Company — Memorandum — November, 13 1876"; vol. 11, file 286-76, "Baker Company — I. G. Baker to Richardson — September 18, 1876," National Archives of Canada, Ottawa; First National Bank of Helena Records, Manuscript Collection 116, file 2-8, "I. G. Baker & Co to Mr. D. C. Corbin — May 1, 1876," MHS. The original contract was signed November 25, 1875, for pay in 1876–77; Klassen, "Baker in Calgary," 47.

CHAPTER 4

1. Schwantes, *Long Day's Journey,* 319–20.

2. *Benton Weekly Record,* January 5, 1877.

3. *Benton Weekly Record,* January 12, 1877.

4. *Benton Weekly Record,* February 23, 1877.

5. *Benton Weekly Record,* March 16 and March 30, 1877.

6. Martin Maginnis Papers, Manuscript Collection 50, file 1, "J. J. Healy to M. Maginnis — 16 February 1875," MHS; Sharp, *Whoop-Up Country,* 219; Francis, "Business, Enterprise and the National Policy," 40–41.

7. *Benton Weekly Record,* June 30, 1876.

8. *Benton Weekly Record,* January 5 and May 11, 1877.

9. *Benton Weekly Record,* April 13 and May 4, 1877; Flanagan, "A Perspective," MHS; Overholser, *Fort Benton,* 94; *River Press,* April 11, 1990; Murphy, *Half Interest in a Silver Dollar,* 22–23, 57, argues that after the Conrads bought into I. G. Baker & Company, Isaac Baker became almost nonexistent in the business. He attributes the formation of the steamboat line and the purchase of the *Red Cloud* to the Conrad brothers. Archival research (several collections at the MHS), however, clearly demonstrates that Isaac Baker is in fact heavily involved with the steamboating aspects of the company.

10. The Howard boatyard built a number of well-known steamers that operated on the Ohio, Mississippi, and Missouri river systems. Fishbaugh, *From Paddle Wheels to Propellers,* 198.

11. National Archives, RG 41, Steamboat Inspection Service, "Proceedings of the Board of Supervising Inspectors of Steam Vessels, 1852–99," Washington, D.C.; *Sunday Courier and Press,* December 16, 1873; Wooldridge, "List of Steamboats"; McDonald, "Missouri River and Its Victims," *Missouri Historical Review* 21 (1927): 591; Fishbaugh, *From Paddle Wheels to Propellers,* 198; Way, *Way's Packet Directory,* 389.

12. While working the Evansville–Tennessee River trade the *Red Cloud*'s master was Allen J. Duncan, with Al Maynard and Joseph Wood serving as clerks. *Evansville Journal,* January 1, 1873; *Sunday Courier and Press,* December 16, 1873; Golden Eagle Club, "All Aboard, July 1948," TMs [photocopy], Ruth Ferris Collection, Herman T. Pott Inland Waterways Library, St. Louis Mercantile Library, St. Louis, Mo.

13. *Benton Weekly Record,* May 14, 1877; Way, *Way's Packet Directory,* 389.

14. National Archives, Public Enrollments from February 12, 1877, to June 29, 1878, RG 41, PE 165, Port of St. Louis, GSA, National Archives, Washington, D.C.; List of Merchant Vessels of the United States, RG 41, series 156, Custom District of New Orleans, Port of St. Louis, GAS, National Archives, Washington, D.C.

15. Hunter, *Steamboats on Western Rivers,* 309–15.

16. *Benton Weekly Record,* April 13, and May 5, 1877.

17. *Benton Weekly Record,* June 1, 1877, reported the boat arrived at Sioux City on May 17.

18. *Bismarck Semi-Weekly Tribune,* May 9, 18, 30, and June 4, 1877.

19. *Bismarck Semi-Weekly Tribune,* June 8, 1877.

20. *Bismarck Semi-Weekly Tribune,* June 15 and 18, 1877.

21. *Bismarck Semi-Weekly Tribune,* June 15, 1877; *River Press,* June 9, 1976; MHS, "Steamboat Arrivals at Fort Benton," *Contributions to the Historical Society of Montana* 3 (1900): 352.

22. Passengers included: A. Blorrin, L. H. Chonquette, Dr. R. A. Wells, Mrs. Wells, Master Richard Wells, Master Ernest Custer Wells, Mrs. J. Moore, Mr. W. G. Conrad, Mrs. W. G. Conrad, Miss Nannie Conrad, Joseph Conrad, A. B. Keeler, Lee Isabelle, Mrs. Lee Isabelle, John Eagler, Mrs. Eagler, Truben, Walstead, F. Aronheiar, Drew, Conors, Neyler, Restley, Hambleton. *Benton Weekly Record,* June 22, 1877.

23. *Bismarck Semi-Weekly Tribune,* June 29, 1877.

24. Memorandum of the steamboat *Red Cloud* Fort Benton to Bismarck June 24–July 11, 1877: "Left Fort Benton June 24th, at 11 A.M., with 225 tons of freight, twenty passengers Co. B, 7th infantry, for Dauphin's Rapids. At the time *Katie P. Kountz* was in port. Met the *Josephine* 20 miles below the mouth of Marias; on the 25th met the *Gen. Custer* ten miles above Cow Island; 26th the *Fannie Tatum* below Poplar River; 27th the *Fancheon* ten miles below Buford, and the *Far West* just behind, the *Mead* at Scott's, the *Fontenelle* below and the *Dugan* at the Slides, the *Nellie Peck* at Little Missouri; 28th the *Durfee* at Berthold. Arrived at Bismarck at 11 A.M. on the 28th." *Bismarck Semi-Weekly Tribune,* June 29, 1877; *Benton Weekly Record,* June 29, 1877; Overholser, *Fort Benton,* 94–97.

25. Robert Craig Wallace Papers, Manuscript Collection 221, file 1-22, "I. G. Baker & Co. to Davis & Wallace, 12 January 1877," "Geo. A. Baker to Davis and Wallace, 12 February 1877," "Geo. A. Baker to Davis and Wallace, 8 March 1877," MHS.

26. *Benton Weekly Record,* May 25, 1877.

27. *Benton Weekly Record,* January 5 and 12, March 4 and 30, 1877; Overholser, *Fort Benton,* 93.

28. Overholser, *Fort Benton,* 93–94.

29. Lass, *History of Steamboating on the Upper Missouri River,* 130–31.

30. *Bismarck Semi-Weekly Tribune,* July 2, 1877.

31. *Bismarck Semi-Weekly Tribune,* July 18, 1877; *Benton Weekly Record,* July 13, 1877.

32. Passengers included: Mr[s]. Sullivan, M. Andersen, Mr. Elberry, Mr. Bird, Mrs. Lewis, Mrs. Moore, Master Hancock, Mr. Crowey, Mr. Barber, Mr. Milbrey, Mr. Wells, Mrs. Lewis, Mrs. Haycock, and Miss Haycock. Memorandum of the steamboat *Red Cloud* Bismarck to Fort Benton July 1877: "Left Bismarck on the morning of the 1st at 9 o'clock. Laid up first night at Big Knife River; second, below the Slide; third, above Tobacco Gardens; fourth, above the mouth of the Yellowstone; fifth, two bends below Poplar Creek; sixth, at Porcupine Creek; seventh, 1st bend below Pochett's grave; eighth,

ran all night without stopping; ninth, laid up at Lone Rapids; tenth, ran all night and arrived at Fort Benton at fifteen minutes before nine on the morning of the 11th, drawing 3 feet 8 inches of water." *Benton Weekly Record,* July 13, 1877.

33. Way, *Way's Packet Directory,* 389; Overholser, *Fort Benton,* 94–97.

34. The memorandum of the trip: "Left Fort Benton evening of the 12th. Boat in Port *Fannie Tatum* and *E. H. Durfee.* Laid up all night at Mollarias; 18th met *Fontenelle* at Hole in the Wall; laid up all night at Hard Scrapple; 14th laid up nine hours for wind. *Josephine* passed up; laid all night at Fort Peck. 11th laid up seven hours in Milk River chute on account of wind; met *Benton* just below; laid up all night above Mo. Muddy; 16th laid up all night at Strawberry Island; 17th met *Mead* above Berthold; *Fletcher* and *Alex Kendall* laid up on account of wind below Stevenson; laid up all night at Dry Point, arrived at Bismarck on the 18th at 4 A.M." *Bismarck Semi-Weekly Tribune,* July 18, 1877.

35. Gov. Wise refers to the boat's pilot. *Bismarck Semi-Weekly Tribune,* July 27, 1877.

36. Passengers included: Miss Kate Conley, Miss B. McHale, Mrs. M. S. Henderson, Mrs. Wells, Mrs. Braum, Mrs. E. S. Moore, Mr. Borastrom, Woods, Dr. D. C. Hill, A. Holbrook, J. E. Lyon, C. W. Grey, G. R. Bell, D. S. Philips, Mr. Kimball, Mr. Rumney, Mr. Glover, Mr. Conley, J. S. Hopps, G. Rittner, L. Murphy, Capt. Thompson, Mr. Cummings, Forester, Captain Benson, Dr. Terry, Mr. McGonigal, and Mr. Tyler. *Benton Weekly Record,* August 3, 1877.

37. Memorandum (log) of the steamboat *Red Cloud* from Fort Benton to Bismarck, July 31–August 7, 1877: "Left Fort Benton, July 31st, 9 P.M.; boats in port; *E. H. Durfee* laid all night at Crocongena. Aug. 1st, laid all night at Gray's wood-yard, twenty miles below Cow Island; scratched rocks all the way down. Aug. 2d, saw plenty of Buffalo on the river; laid all night below Pochett's grave. Aug. 3d, laid all night below Wolf Point. Aug. 4th, laid all night at Red Butte. Aug. 5th, met *Benton* fifty miles below Buford; laid all night at Little Knife river. Aug. 6th, met *Western* at mouth of Little Missouri, and *Far West* below Berthold; laid all night at Big Knife river. Aug. 7th, arrived at Bismarck at 12 m. drawing three feet and carrying sixty passengers." *Bismarck Semi-Weekly Tribune,* August 8, 1877.

38. *Bismarck Semi-Weekly Tribune,* July 16, 1877.

39. Berry, *Whoop-Up Trail,* 34, 45.

40. *Benton Weekly Record,* January 12, 1877; Overholser, *Fort Benton,* 96.

41. *Benton Weekly Record,* April 13, 1877.

CHAPTER 5

1. *Benton Weekly Record,* July 20, 1882.

2. National Archives, 1877, Public Enrollments from February 12, 1877, to June 29, 1878, RG 41, PE 105, Port of St. Louis, GSA, National Archives, Washington, D.C. This record indicates that a change was made in the shape of the boat's bow. Photographic evidence, however, does not support this. *Benton Weekly Record,* March 6, 1878.

3. The Bismarck paper reported that the departure date was April 1, and that the boat drew 34 inches. *Benton Weekly Record,* March 29, 1878; *Bismarck Tri-Weekly Tribune,* April 9, 1878.

4. The *Nellie Peck* was a stern-wheel packet built in Brownsville, Pennsylvania, in 1871 for Durfee & Peck. The boat was often commanded by Captain Grant Marsh. During the freighting season of 1878 the boat was leased to run in the Baker Line. Way, *Way's Packet Directory,* 342.

5. The Benton Transportation Company (T. C. Power & Brother) was offering second-class fares at $51. *Benton Weekly Record,* April 19, 1878.

6. Overholser, *Fort Benton,* 97–98.

7. *Benton Weekly Record,* April 5, 1878.

8. Overholser, *Fort Benton,* 98.

9. *Benton Weekly Record,* April 26, and May 3, 1878.

10. This incident demonstrates the moment to moment difficulties encountered with navigating the Missouri. Even after significant modifications the boat struggled. *Benton Weekly Record,* May 10, 1878.

11. Passengers on the *Red Cloud: Gentlemen's Cabin*—J. D. Smith, Mr. Patterson, Wm. Bloom, John H. Bolton, Jas. H. Hall, James J. Lee, Henry W. Gebaner, J. F. Devinna, Herman Greimer, and Mr. O'Connell. *Ladies Cabin*—J. H. Matthews and lady, Mrs. MacDonald and two children, Mrs. L. E. Bloom, Mrs. Yeager and four children, Mr. Marshall, Miss Marshall, Mrs. O'Connell and three children, Miss La Croix, Mrs. Fant and two children, Mrs. S. Q. Gorden, Miss Anna Lochrer, Miss Carrie Lochrer, Mrs. Goodrich, Mr. Wetzel, lady and child, Mrs. Galbith, Mr. Lampton, lady and two children, Mrs. Connley and two children, Mrs. Foster, three children and nurse, Mr. Wetzel and mother, and Mrs. Eliza Sloan. *Deck Passengers*—Wm. B. Johnson, Isabel Johnson, Thomas Sharp, J. L. Learengood and wife, J. Learengood, Wm. Gilbert, B. Y. Bailey, Lewis Johnson, Wm. Ethridge, W. Cunningham, Mr. Kermode, J. Hurtz and family, Mrs. Heik, Miss Heik, Chas. Lippert, Aug Beckman and wife, Jas. Gilliland, Mr. Richards and family, two horses and one wagon, D. C. Ward, Wm. Gulick, Newton Johnson, S. Hallgarth, Jno Parish, Jacob Clark, Emma Johnson. *Benton Weekly Record,* April 26, and May 17, 1878.

12. Serving with Captain Massie for the 1878 season were Al Maynard, clerk; Boone and Scurry, pilots; and Paul Murphy, mate. *Bismarck Tri-Weekly Tribune,* April 12, 1878; *Benton Weekly Record,* May 17, 1878.

13. Berry, *The Whoop-Up Trail,* 33.

14. Denny, *Law Marches West,* 141.

15. I. G. Baker & Compnay actually won its first Canadian beef contract in 1875 to supply Fort Calgary, but the firm sublet this contract to a man named Shaw who thus becomes the first American to supply beef to the Canadian West. Baker & Company would not actually supply beef until they won the 1877–78 Indian and NWMP contracts. First National Bank of Helena Records, Manuscript Collection 116, file 2-8, "Letter from I. G. Baker & Co. to Mr. D. C. Corbin—22 May 1876," MHS; Berry, *The Whoop-Up Trail,* 34, 46.

16. Breen, *Canadian Prairie West and the Ranching Frontier,* 15.

17. *Bismarck Tri-Weekly Tribune,* May 31, 1878.

18. Passengers on the *Red Cloud* included: Wm McDuff and wife, Mrs. Wells and two children, C. S. Ashby, wife and nurse, Mrs. Hawkins, Miss Mollie Conrad, Miss Maggie Carroll, Mrs. Capt. Williams and daughter, Charles E. Conrad, Matt Carroll, Col. Fred White, Maj. J. M. Walsh, Henry R. Flemming, Frank Straub, W. H. Ulen, Chas. Seaman, John Denn, Thos. Forney, G. P. Asher, W. Arnold, D. Horan, C. Caskilly, W. Lynn, F. Leslie, W. E. Morgan, G. B. Moffett, I. Morton, I. McNeel, I. A. K. Mountain, Wm. McRae, H. Morehead, W. H. McAlpine, John McMillan, I. G. McClellaw, J. M. McFarland, K. McQueen, A Moleson, G. Mowat, J. Ownens, J. T. O'Keeth, F. O'Connor, Jas Pringle, J. M. Robinson, Thos. Green, Jerry Keathing, John Eyeler, Henry hartman, Martin Lawson, Wm. Fally, Wm. McClain, W. L. Wilson, W. T. Richeson, H. Watkins,

J. Mead, G. S. Blake, G. Curtis, C. Link, Jas. Phillips, John Huff, G. Arnold, B. F. Lewis, T. McCally, M. Hardy, Aug Shraeder, Dan Cowley, John Burke, Wm. Meeker, Lewis Walsh, Frank Parks, James Harris, R. Wild, G. Wells, W. R. Wright, G. Webb, H. Wilson, W. J. Wilson, J. A. Werkin, P. S. Vancourtland, T. Thompson, Wm. Taite, H. Tourney, A Telee, W. D. Smith, C. Steward, T. Smith, T. H. Scofield, A. B. Simmons, A. T. Gilmore, T. Grant, G. Gamsby, A. Frazier, G. Teason, R. Fletcher, W. A. Fitzsimmons, T. Ford, Chas. Ereitinger, T. F. Ecklin, F. J. Devlin, J. Davis, H. Deminally, W. Chamberlain, J. Crozier, T. Conrad, D. Craig, E. B. Cook, J. M. Bliss, D. C. Byers, F. W. Butler, Wm. Byers, W. D. Beaty;—the final 60 names were recruits of the North West Mounted Police that were left at the mouth of the Marias. *Benton Weekly Record,* June 14, 1878.

19. Memorandum of the steamboat *Red Cloud* Fort Benton to Bismarck, June 11, 1878: "Left Fort Benton June 11th 9 P.M.; laid up for the night above the Mouth Marias; 12th met *Benton* at Carroll 3 P.M. *Rosebud* ten miles below Fort Hawley 7 P.M.; laid up for the night ten miles above Pocket Point; 13th met *Big Horn* at Amelia Poe 4 P.M.; laid up for the night at Sander's wood yard below Wolf Point; 17th met *Fontenelle* at Big Muddy above Buford 10 A.M.; *Nellie Peck* at Big Muddy below Buford 5 P.M.; laid up for the night at Strawberry Island; 15 met *Key West* and *Josephine* at Fort Berthold at 6 A.M.; *Helena* at McCauley's coal banks 9:30 A.M.; arrived at Bismarck 2 P.M." *Bismarck Tri-Weekly Tribune,* June 21, 1878.

20. *Bismarck Tri-Weekly Tribune,* June 21, 1878.

21. *Benton Weekly Record,* July 5, 1878; *Bismarck Tri-Weekly Tribune,* July 5, 1878.

22. Overholser, *Fort Benton,* 94–97.

23. *Bismarck Tri-Weekly Tribune,* July 12, 1878; Way, *Way's Packet Directory,* 389.

24. The boat name appears as the *Colonel Macleod,* the *Col. MacLeod,* and the *Col. McLeod.* It is specified as the latter on its enrollment records and, in a letter dated February 16, 1925, from I. P. Baker to W. J. MacDonald of the Steamboat Inspection Service, Baker informs MacDonald that the correct spelling is *Col. McLeod.* Isaac P. Baker Papers, Small Collection 387, MHS. No photographs are known to exist for this vessel for verification. However, newspapers of the time advertised the boat as the *Col. Macleod.*

25. *Benton Weekly Record,* May 10, 1878; Way, *Way's Packet Directory,* 104; Overholser, *Fort Benton,* 99; Murphy, *Half Interest in a Silver Dollar,* 58.

26. *Benton Weekly Record,* August 30, and October 25, 1878; Overholser, *Fort Benton,* 105.

27. *Annual Report of the Chief of Engineers, 1879,* part 2, 1095; Lass, *History of Steamboating on the Upper Missouri,* 132; Overholser, *Fort Benton,* 99.

28. Sharp, *Whoop-Up Country,* 214.

CHAPTER 6

1. *Benton Weekly Record,* April 25, 1879.

2. Passengers on the steamboat *Red Cloud: Cabin Passengers*—W. Conway, F. Leavengood, N. Blair, C. Reeves, F. Holloway, T. Engles, H. Mason, Geo C. Davis, B. F. Wilson, H. Sutherland, wife and son, Mrs. E. Connolly and three children, O. Wilson, wife and two children, Mrs. West and four children, Mrs. Kent and son, T. Hubbord, John Semple, Mrs. Frank Jackony and five children, Mrs. King, child and son, Dr. Merrill U S A, Mrs. Merrill, C. Baker, F. McCary, J. Vanhook, F. Churchill, C. Price, M. Gardiner, wife and child, Mrs. McCrary and child, Joseph Baker, Mrs. Boyle, two children and servant, Mrs. Alice Street and child, Miss Baker, A. Wickerd, Joe Culbertsen, wife and child,

Mattie Bell and two children, M. Wethington, O. Burns, J. Britt, Frank Miller, J. Merry, Wm. Puffer, D. Smiley, J. Nesbit and wife, J. Ownes and wife, C. Powell, E. Creely, W. Boyle, Cherokee and friend. *Deck Passengers*—G. Watson, A. LaPea, T. Doan, J. Cavenaugh, L. Felix, M. Curry and wife, E. Holm, H. Lanken, A. Bruitt, Mrs. Jacobs and five children, A. Brana, wife and three children, A. Jacobs, D. Tressler, M. Vance, I. Martin, W. Brown, L. Jobas, P. Walker, J. Curry, J. Wise, Messrs: Ostroon, Ferguson, Brand, Hartsborn, Gill, Boyd, Farrenhart, Taylor, Gibbs, Heagen, Randall, Rolley, Lenden, Flynn, and Keefer. *Benton Weekly Record,* May 16, 1879.

3. Members of the Gardner family who traveled on the *Red Cloud* included Edward Morgan Gardner, age thirty-seven; Flora McCreary Baker Gardner, age forty; Rachel Ross McCreary, age sixty-six; Florence R. Baker, age twenty-one; Charles F. Baker, age twenty; Joseph Edwin Baker, age thirteen; Archie Russell Gardner, age eight; Mary Waterman Gardner, age seven; Mattie Jeanette Gardner, age four; and Finley McCreary, age unknown—a cousin of the other children. The family spent the night on the *Red Cloud* when it landed in Benton and then took a wagon trail to Bozeman, Montana, where they settled. A brief account of the river journey was kept by Edward Gardner, Diary 1879, Small Collection 734, MHS. Descendants of the Gardener family retraced the 1879 trip on the *Red Cloud* as part of a family reunion in 1979. *River Press,* July 25, 1979.

4. Saum, "Stanley Huntley Interviews Sitting Bull," *Montana: The Magazine of Western History,* 32, no. 2 (1982): 6–7. Saum's article discusses the debate concerning the legitimacy of Huntley's Sitting Bull interview and the speculation concerning the interview.

5. *Benton Weekly Record,* June 13, 1879.

6. Passengers on the steamboat *Red Cloud:* Col. Macleod, L. N. F. Crozier, Capt. Dalrymple Clark, Capt. John Cotton, Constable Norman, Hon. E. Dewdney, T. Wright, Mrs. Boos, Ed Boos, Miss Carrie Boos, Mrs. Dillon, Miss Addie Dillon, Miss Mamie Dillon, Mrs. Kitty Branthaven, Chas. Conrad, Mrs. Hawkins, Miss Alice Conrad, Jos. Conrad, J. W. Conrad, Mrs. Conrad, Mrs. McCabe, J. P. McCabe, Mrs. Barker, Frank Purcell, D. Keelu, H. J. Taylor, R. W. Gawsen, and 100 Canadian Mounted Police. *Benton Weekly Record,* June 13, 1879.

7. RG 18, series B, vol. 2186 (reel T-6269), "Letters," August 10, 1881, National Archives of Canada, Ottawa.

8. Overholser, *Fort Benton,* 103–104.

9. *Press and Dakotaian,* May 5, 1879; Overholser, *Fort Benton,* 102–108.

10. *Benton Weekly Record,* November 22, 1878; Flanagan, "A Perspective"; Oviatt, "Fort Benton, River Capital," 153.

11. Greenhood, Bohm & Co. Records, Manuscript Collection 130, file 1-2, "I. G. Baker & Co. to Greenhood, Bohm & Co.," July 21, 1879, MHS.

12. Richard Lockey Papers, Manuscript Collection 227, file 3-1, "I. G. Baker & Co. to Richard Lockey," August 6, 1879; September 11, 1879; September 17, 1879; September 19, 1879, MHS.

13. National Archives, RG 393, entry 1292, Quartermaster Records, Letters Received, box 2(1879), "Contract, 28 March 1879"; RG 92, entry 225, Quartermaster Records, Consolidated Correspondence, box 398, "Conrad, Charles, 25 May 1883," Washington, D.C.

14. Thomas C. Power Papers, Manuscript Collection 55, file 276-35, "T. C. Power *vs.* I. G. Baker, 1 July 1881; 15 October 1883," MHS; *Benton Weekly Record,* July 21,1881; Overholser, *Fort Benton,* 105.

15. Overholser, *Fort Benton,* 103–104.

16. *Benton Weekly Record,* March 19,1880; Berry, *The Whoop-Up Trail,* 47.

17. The following excerpt is a reminiscence from one of those past journal entries and experiences. It is included in its entirety here because of the vast amount of information she details about the *Red Cloud* and life associated with its operation. Her papers are located at Montana State University–Bozeman, Merrill G. Burlingame Special Collections, Lou Stocking Stewart Papers, 1871–1941, Collection 339 and Small Collection 795, MHS.

18. Stewart, "Up-River on the *Red Cloud,*" Reminiscence ca. 1937, Small Collection 339, MHS; Murphy, *Half Interest in a Silver Dollar,* 9–12.

19. *Benton Weekly Record,* May 14, 1880.

20. Passengers on the *Red Cloud:* J. A. Vale, J. Humes, M. Billedo, F. Wies, Miss Wies, R. S. Ford, M. Arboet, O. Mayley, Mrs. Kanouse and two daughters, M. Clay and wife and child, Mrs. Isabel and four children, N. Hudson, Mrs. Hopkins, Mrs. Patterson and two children, Mrs. Berry and five children, M. Barnard, A. Allison, M. Harrison, W. Waston, I. V. Stanley, Geo. Calvert, Jos. A. Aker, Mr. Cullen and wife and six children, Mrs. Wilston, Miss Lou Stocking, Mrs. Miller and daughter, J. S. Rice and wife and two children and servant, Wm. Kerry, A. Seldon, G. Wallace, G. D. Smilley and wife and two children and servant, R. H. Ellcote, W. L. Hickman, Wm. Smith, O. Ausorth, C. Barker, B. Sanderson and wife, Mary Sanderson, Lucy Morton, Verrian Morton, Margret Hoge, James Matkin, Willis Matkin, D. Sanders and wife and two children, Kot Ragan, J. H. Sirfeat and wife and two children, Simon Freeze and wife, D. Lefore. *Benton Weekly Record,* June 11, 1880.

21. *Benton Weekly Record,* June 18 and 25,1880.

22. Overholser, *Fort Benton,* 105–106.

23. *Benton Weekly Record,* March 9, 1880; Overholser, *Fort Benton,* 106.

24. Passengers on the *Red Cloud:* Mrs. Hinton and two children and servant, Dr. H. J. Coffroth, Col. A. B. McDonald—Inspt. N. W. M. Police, Capt. J. H. Baldwin and wife and child, J. C. Nelson, S. F. Peckham, David Hill and wife, J. W. McCay and wife, Mrs. Rosencrane, C. H. Bushel, R. H. Sherwin, D. A. Cory, C. Edwards and son, Blaisdel wife and son, D. E. Folsom and wife, B. H. Jones and wife, Miss Jennie Bates, Miss Belle Tucker, J. C. Levi, Richard Sample, Edward Peck, D. Prosser and wife, Mrs. McClutchie, Mrs. Cox and daughter, Edward Pesk, D. R. Kellog, J. Blair, W. McMeans, J. C. Monger, W. M. Monger, Henry Elder, P. McEntire, C. C. Lanning, P. W. Scott, M. McAfee, Chas. Lucry, M. Perchaet, Wm. Cochran, R. M. boyle, Richard Smith, Ed Markham and wife, Kenel Markham, Sarah Markham, Minnie Markham, M. Reagan, Joseph Donns, N. C. Grant, Robert Miller, P. Morrison, Geo. McCortney, I. T. Brngrees, J. Sholtz, W. Bliss, P. R. Worthington, J. B. Jacriss, J. E. Jacriss, Geo. Lindsley, Geo. Mills, Leopold Vandell, E. Miller. *Benton Weekly Record,* July 9, 1880.

25. *Benton Weekly Record,* July 9, 1880; *River Press,* October 6, 1943.

26. The boat arrived with George A. Williams as master and L. L. Hine as clerk. *Benton Weekly Record,* July 23, 1880.

27. Overholser, *Fort Benton,* 107.

28. West, "Coulson and the Clark's Fork Bottom," *Montana: The Magazine of Western History* 35, no. 4 (1985): 54; Overholser, *Fort Benton,* 107–109.

29. Thomas C. Power Papers, Manuscript Collection 55, file 228-7, "Freight Bill, 24 March 1881," MHS.

30. Thomas C. Power Papers, Manuscript Collection 55, file 91-6, 19 April 1881, MHS.

31. Thomas C. Power Papers, Manuscript Collection 55, file 84-4, 28 May 1881, MHS.

32. Sharp, *Whoop-Up Country,* 224.

33. Thomas C. Power Papers, Manuscript Collection 55, file 273-42, "Agreement between I. G. Baker & Co. and T. C. Power & Bro., 18 January 1881," MHS.

34. Klassen, "I. G. Baker & Company in Calgary," 49; see also Francis, "Montana Business and Canadian Regionalism in the 1870s and 1880s," 296, and Francis, "Business, Enterprise and the National Policy," 25–28.

35. Klassen, "I. G. Baker & Co.," 49.

36. These agreements extended into almost every facet of both firms' business, including Canadian and American contracts. Thomas C. Power Papers, Manuscript Collection 55, file 273-42, "Agreement, 1 February 1882"; "Agreement, 14 March 1882"; file 273-28, "Agreement, 23 April 1881"; file 274-2, "Agreement, nd 1882"; "Agreement, 14 February 1883"; "Agreement, 5 June 1885," MHS.

37. Thomas C. Power Papers, Manuscript Collection 55, file 228-7, "Receipt, 14 March 1882," MHS.

38. Overholser, *Fort Benton,* 110–11.

39. *River Press,* April 27, 1881.

40. Passengers on the steamboat *Red Cloud:* W. B. Settle and wife and child, Mrs. Nora Connelly, Mrs. Anderson and son, W. J. Stevenson, B. I. Rotwell, Mrs. Rotwell, S. B. Price, Joh Price, John Ray, Mrs. Ray, P. H. Leary, W. M. Hines, Benj. Spets, D. W. Cutney, B. Kenphan, Geo. Miller, I. McDaniel, J. M. McMinner, Benj. Arnold, Mrs. Hicks, Sallie Treadwell, and Julia Davis. *Benton Weekly Record,* June 9, 1881; *River Press,* June 1, 1881; Overholser, *Fort Benton,* 109–13.

41. *Benton Weekly Record,* June 9, 1881.

42. *Benton Weekly Record,* June 16, 1881.

43. *River Press,* June 15, 1881.

44. Overholser, *Fort Benton,* 111.

45. *Benton Weekly Record,* June 30, 1881.

46. Passengers on the steamboat *Red Cloud:* Col. Cochrane, Dr. McEachran, Mr. Ginns, Major Baynes, Mr. Thompson and Mr. Wilson of the Cochrane Cattle Co., Captain Clark—U.S.A., Hon. J. E. Wiser, W. F. Lewis, Dr. Greenleaf and wife and three children and servant, J. E. Chipman, Mr. Lyon, Mrs. Porter and two children, Mr. Hyndeman and wife, A. Brickman, Mr. McCaffey, W. Hannah, L. Hannah, M. Hannah, Spearson and wife, John Lanfest, W. B. Shunk, and Mr. Shott. *Benton Weekly Record,* June 30, 1881.

47. *Benton Weekly Record,* June 30, 1881.

48. Passengers on the steamboat *Red Cloud:* Mr. Pye and Master Harry Pye, Miss Fanny Hopkins, Miss Anna McKinna of St. Louis, Miss Holmes, Miss Nurray, Miss McDonald, Judge Napton of Missouri, G. W. Casey, and 3 officers and 4 Northwest Mounted Police recruits headed for Fort Walsh. *Benton Weekly Record,* July 28, 1881. When The *Red Cloud* left Bismarck it actually carried sixty-two horses bound for Fort Walsh, sixty for the NWMP, and two for private individuals at Fort Walsh, all of which were to be dropped at Coal Banks. Only sixty horses were put off the steamer at that location, however, since one horse was lost while driving and another was left at Fort Claggett, lame.

49. *Benton Weekly Record,* July 28, 1881.

50. *Benton Weekly Record,* August 11 and 25, September 8, 22, and 29, 1881.

51. Joel Overholser Files, Montana Agriculture Museum, Fort Benton, Montana.

52. Thomas C. Power Papers, Manuscript Collection 55, file 84-4, "Agreement-18 January 1881"; file 273-28, "Agreement—12 September 1881," MHS; *Benton Weekly Record,* October 6, 1881; Berry, *The Whoop-Up Trail,* 34; Francis, "Business, Enterprise, and the National Policy," 28.

53. It is curious that T. C. Power would agree to the store trade/buyout unless they were not privy to the information that the NWMP would soon be abandoning the Walsh post. RG 18, vol. 1004, file 65, "Contract," January 24, 1883, Canadian National Archives, Ottawa; Thomas C. Power Papers, Manuscript Collection 55, file 84-4, January 18, 1881, MHS; *River Press,* April 5, 1882.

CHAPTER 7

1. Thomas C. Power Papers, Manuscript Collection 55, file 273-42, "Agreement, 1 February 1882," MHS.

2. *River Press,* March 8, 1882; *Benton Weekly Record,* March 9, 1882.

3. RG 18, series B-3, vol. 2186 (reel T-6269), "Letters," May 24, 1882, Canadian National Archives, Ottawa.

4. *Benton Weekly Record,* April 6, 1882; RG 18, vol. 1009, file 546a, "1883," September 5, 1883, Canadian National Archives, Ottawa.

5. RG 18, series B-3, vol. 2186 (reel T-6269), "Letters," April 30, 1882, Canadian National Archives, Ottawa.

6. The *Key West* was a stern-wheel packet built in Pittsburgh in 1871. The boat was owned primarily by John Todd and Nicholas Buison. The boat made a total of twenty-three trips to various Montana points during its career, most as a leased boat with the Baker Line, the Coulson Line, and the American Fur Company. In 1882, Joe Todd served as master. The *Wyoming* was a stern-wheel packet built in Sewickley, Pennsylvania, in 1879. This was a very large steamer, rated at 1,034 tons, that actually made only one trip to Fort Benton during its entire career. It arrived at Fort Benton on June 25, 1882, with 600 tons of freight. It returned downriver with 316 head of cattle, the largest export of cattle by steamboat out of Fort Benton ever recorded. The boat typically operated in the Coulson Line. *River Press,* May 10 and 17, 1882; Way, *Way's Packet Directory,* 271, 492; Overholser, *Fort Benton,* 118–19.

7. The *General Terry* was a stern-wheel packet built in Freedom, Pennsylvania, in 1878. The boat was originally built for John Todd (note above) and W. A. Burleigh of Miles City, Montana, but they had financial trouble when it came time to pay for the boat. Ultimately, the boat changed hands several times over its career. In 1882 the boat was owned by the Peck Line along with the now familiar *Nellie Peck* and was often leased to I. G. Baker & Company. *River Press,* May 10, 1882; Way, *Way's Packet Directory,* 183–84; Overholser, *Fort Benton,* 118–19.

8. *Benton Weekly Record,* April 20, 1882.

9. Overholser, *Fort Benton,* 118.

10. *River Press,* March 15, 1882.

11. *River Press,* May 17 and 31, 1882.

12. *Benton Weekly Record,* April 6, 1882.

13. The first trip in 1882 was difficult for the *Red Cloud;* the boat was laid up for a couple of weeks near Nebraska City while awaiting repairs for a burst cylinder head and then again outside of Sioux City for low water. *River Press,* April 9 and 11, 1882; *Benton*

Weekly Record, April 13, 1882. Passengers on the steamboat *Red Cloud:* Ms. Sage and the Misses Sage, Mrs. Hanley and two children, Tom Burke, Frank Bulien, Mrs. Long and family, Thomas Walden, A. J. Bright and family, W. O. Walden, Mrs. Lizzie Brown, F. R. Smith, G. A. Wolfe and family, J. E. Murphy, Wm. Downs, 205 Mounted Police recruits that were put off at Coal Banks and over one hundred deck passengers for Benton. *River Press,* June 7, 1882; *Benton Weekly Record,* May 25 and June 8, 1882.

14. Two of the recruits that boarded the *Red Cloud* in Bismarck never made it to Coal Banks. Both men were reported (one presumed) drowned in the Missouri River prior to arrival at Coal Banks. RG 18, series B-3, vol. 2186 (reel T-6269), "Letters," June 5, 1882; June 16, 1882, Canadian National Archives, Ottawa.

15. *River Press,* July 7, 1882; Overholser, *Fort Benton,* 116–18; Flanagan, "A Perspective," MHS.

16. After scouring the Benton papers covering a year after the arrival of the immigrants I could find no mention that Patrick ever returned to Fort Benton. *Benton Weekly Record,* June 8, 1882.

17. Passengers on the steamboat *Red Cloud:* James Millen, James McDonald, William Green, P. Ryan, I. N. Vail. Lieut. Fredericks, W. M. Byington, Thomas Cushing, John Claymo, G. W. Gautz, Charles Buckman and Wm. Slanks. *River Press,* June 28, 1882; *Benton Weekly Record,* June 29, 1882.

CHAPTER 8

1. *Benton Weekly Record,* July 20, 1882.

2. *Benton Weekly Record,* July 19, 1882.

3. The telegrams sent by I. G. Baker and T. J. Todd were printed in the local newspaper to help keep the citizens of Benton informed. The original telegrams were not relocated by the author. *Benton Weekly Record,* July 19, 1882.

4. *Benton Weekly Record,* July 20, 1882.

5. Corbin, "Shifting Sand and Muddy Water," 91; Way, *Way's Packet Directory,* 383.

6. I. G. Baker & Company Papers, Small Collection 293, file 1, "Isaac G. Baker to Charles and William Conrad, February 13, 1883," MHS.

7. T. C. Power and the Fort Benton Transportation Company made arrangements with I. G. Baker & Company to carry 500 tons of Baker's 1883 Fort Benton, Canadian, and Indian freight, any remaining freight could be shipped via Coulson. This allowed the majority of the freighting revenue to stay with a Montana firm for the 1883 season rather than the lower river Coulson firm. Thomas C. Power Papers, Manuscript Collection 55, file 15-30, MHS.

8. Thomas C. Power Papers, Manuscript Collection 55, file 274-5, "Testimonial, August 11, 1883," MHS.

9. Flanagan, "A Perspective," MHS.

10. Ibid.

11. Sharp, "Merchant Princes of the Plains," 20.

12. *Benton Weekly Record,* August 18, 1883.

13. Sharp, *Whoop-Up Country,* 300.

14. Overholser, *Fort Benton,* 119–20.

15. T. C. Power Papers, Manuscript Collection 55, file 129-3, June 8, 1883, MHS; Francis, "Business, Enterprise, and the National Policy," 62.

16. Sharp, "Merchant Princes of the Plains," 20.

17. Burns & Eliot, *Calgary, Her Industry and Resources,* 27.
18. *Tribune,* December 16, 1906; Sharp, *Whoop-Up Country,* 210.
19. *Benton Weekly Record,* September 3, 1890.
20. Overholser, *Fort Benton,* 127.
21. Sharp, "Merchant Princes of the Plains," 20; Flanagan, "A Perspective," MHS, 28, 30.
22. *Helena Independent,* June 8, 1920; Murphy, *Half Interest in a Silver Dollar,* 60, notes that the boat lay derelict after the sinking until it was finally broken up in the 1883 spring rise, scattering the boat's remains down the Missouri. Only the boat's upper works would have been sent downriver, a common phenomenon suffered by sunken boats in the Missouri—the hulls settled into the sandy bottom and the upper decks would eventually break up and wash away, leaving the hull and cargoes intact in the mud below.
23. Corbin, "Shifting Sand and Muddy Water," 91.
24. Malone, Roeder, and Lang, *Montana,* 296–302; Malone and Etulain, *American West: A Twentieth Century History,* 98, 228; Sandon and Sullivan, "Taming the Missouri and Treating Depression," *Montana: The Magazine of Western History* 27, no. 3 (1977): 34–57.
25. Corbin, "Shifting Sand and Muddy Water," 91.
26. Ibid.

APPENDIX A

1. Newspaper accounts make this date, June 10, 1880, as the first arrival of the *Red Cloud* at Fort Benton for the season. Ms. Stewart is on the passenger list for June 10. *Benton Weekly Record,* June 11, 1880.
2. Stewart, "Up-River on the 'Red Cloud,'" Reminiscence ca. 1937, Small Collection 795, MHS; Murphy, *Half Interest in a Silver Dollar,* 9–12.

APPENDIX B

1. *Benton Weekly Record,* June 9, 1881.

Bibliography

ARCHIVES AND MANUSCRIPTS

Annual Report of the Chief of Engineers, 1879. United States Army, Washington, D.C. National Archives, Washington, D.C.

Ashby, Shirley Carter. "Diary." Small Collection 283, Montana Historical Society, Helena.

Chouteau-Papin Collection. Missouri Historical Society Archives, St. Louis, Missouri.

Baker, Isaac G. "Untitled Papers, 1848–1856." Unpublished papers and letters, Missouri Historical Society Archives, St. Louis, Missouri.

———. Vertical File, Montana Historical Society, Helena.

Baker, Isaac P. "Papers 1923–1925." Small Collection 378, Montana Historical Society, Helena.

Chittenden, Hiram Martin. "List of Steamboat Wrecks in the Missouri River from the Beginning of Steamboat Navigation to the Present Time." *Annual Report of the Chief of Engineers, U.S. Army,* Serial Set 3631–3636 (1897). Washington, D.C.

Conrad, Charles E. "Papers." Small Collection 340, Montana Historical Society, Helena.

First National Bank of Helena. "Records." Manuscript Collection 116, Montana Historical Society, Helena.

Flanagan, May G. "A Perspective on the Life and Times of I. G. Baker [1940s]." Tms [photocopy], May G. Flanagan Papers, Small Collection 1236, Montana Historical Society, Helena.

Gardner, Edward M. "Diary, 1879." Small Collection 734, Montana Historical Society, Helena.

Golden Eagle Club. "All Aboard, July 1948," Tms [photocopy], Ruth Ferris Collection, Herman T. Pott Inland Waterways Library, St. Louis Mercantile Library, St. Louis, Missouri.

Greenhood, Bohm & Co. "Records." Manuscript Collection 130, Montana Historical Society, Helena.

Howell, Charles W. "Letter to General A. A. Humphreys from Colonel J. H. Macomb forwarding the Report of the Upper Missouri River conducted by Major C. W. Howell, in nine parts, January 14 1868." Records of the Office of the Chief of Engineers, Correspondence Division, entry 25, Letters Received, 1865–1870, box 17-18, no. 641, RG 77. National Archives, Washington, D.C.

Hudson's Bay Company Records. "Peigan Post 1833–1883." Glenbow-Alberta Institute, Calgary.

I. G. Baker & Co. "Papers." Small Collection 293, Montana Historical Society, Helena.

List of Merchant Vessels of the United States, RG 41, series 156, Custom District of New Orleans, Port of St. Louis, Missouri. National Archives, Washington, D.C.

Lockey, Richard. "Papers." Manuscript Collection 227, Montana Historical Society, Helena.

Maginnis, Martin. "Papers." Manuscript Collection 50, Montana Historical Society, Helena.

Map of the Missouri River from its Mouth to Three Forks, Montana, 1892–1897. In eighty-four sheets and nine index sheets, Missouri River Commission, RG 77, Civil Works Map File, 930 Portfolio Map. National Archives, Washington, D.C.

Mullan, John. "Report on the Construction of a Military Road from Fort Walla-Walla to Fort Benton." *Senate Documents,* 37 Cong., 2 sess., Doc. 43 (1853). Washington, D.C.

National Archives of Canada, Ottawa. RG 18 (North-West Mounted Police), series A-1, vol. 4, file 98-75, "Statement of Mr. I. G. Baker, Fort Benton, Montana, 25 February 1875."

———. RG 18, series A-1, vol. 9, file 92-76, "Baker & Co.—1876."

———. RG 18, series A-1, vol. 10, file 170-76, "Contract for supply of pay from Baker & Co. 1876–77."

———. RG 18, series A-1, vol. 11, file 248-76, "Baker Company—Memorandum 13 November 1876."

———. RG 18, series B-3, vol. 2186 (reel T-6269), "Letters," July 24, 1881; August 10, 1881; October 10, 1881; April 30, 1882; May 24, 1882; June 5, 1882; June 16, 1882.

———. RG 18, vol. 1004, file 65, "Contract," January 24, 1883.

———. RG 18, vol. 1009, file 546a, "1883," September 5, 1883.

———. *Sessional Papers,* No. 188, Victoria A, 1879.

———. *Macdonald Papers,* vol. 518, Macdonald to Cartier, June 16, 1871.

———. *Macdonald Papers,* vol. 252, Morris to Macdonald, November 16, 1872 and January 17, 1873.

———. *Alexander Campbell Papers,* S. L. Tilley to Campbell, December 3, 1872.

Overholser, Joel. Files. Montana Agriculture Museum, Fort Benton.

P. Chouteau Maffitt Collection, Missouri Historical Society Archives, St. Louis, Missouri.

Power, Thomas C. "Papers." Manuscript Collection 55, Montana Historical Society, Helena.

Proceedings of the Board of Supervising Inspectors of Steam Vessels, 1852–99. RG 41, Steamboat Inspection Service, Washington, D.C. National Archives, Washington, D.C.

Public Enrollments. February 12, 1877 to June 29, 1878, RG 41, PE 105, Port of St. Louis, Missouri. National Archives, Washington, D.C.

———. February 12, 1877 to June 29, 1878, RG 41, PE 165, Port of St. Louis, Missouri. National Archives, Washington, D.C.

Quarter Master Records, Letters Received, RG 393, entry 1292, box 2 (1879). National Archives, Washington, D.C.

Quarter Master Records, Consolidated Correspondence, RG 92, entry 225, box 398. National Archives, Washington, D.C.

Raynolds, W. F. "Report on the Exploration of the Yellowstone River." *Annual Report of the Chief of Engineers, U.S. Army (1868).* Washington, D.C.

Stewart, Lou Stocking. "Papers 1871–1941." Collection 339, Merrill G. Burlingame Special Collections, Montana State University Library, Montana State University, Bozeman.

———. "Up-River on the *Red Cloud.*" Small Collection 795, Montana Historical Society Archives, Helena.

Sublette Papers. Missouri Historical Society Archives, St. Louis, Missouri.

Trail, E. B. "Scrapbooks." E. B. Trail Collection (#2071), vol. 41, Western Historical

Manuscript Collection, Joint Collections of the University of Missouri and the State Historical Society of Missouri, University of Missouri, Columbia.

Wallace, Robert Craig. "Papers." Manuscript Collection 221, Montana Historical Society, Helena.

Werner, Elmer. Letter from Great Falls, Montana to Ralph Arnold, February 11, 1928. Vertical File-Steamboats-Montana, Montana Historical Society Archives, Montana Historical Society, Helena.

Wheatley, William M. Letter from Gravis Mill, Missouri, to John Wheatley, March 18, 1866. Robert W. Binkley Collection, London, Ontario.

Wooldridge, Fielding L. "Lists of Steamboats Compiled by Fielding L. Wooldridge." Unpublished manuscript in four volumes [1930], Herman T. Potts Inland Waterways Library, St. Louis Mercantile Library, St. Louis, Missouri.

BOOKS AND ARTICLES

Albright, Robert E. "The Relations of Montana with the Federal Government, 1864–1889." Ph.D. diss., Stanford University, 1939.

Anonymous, ed. *History of Montana, 1739–1885.* Chicago: Warner, Beers & Co., 1885.

———. *Progressive Men of the State of Montana.* Chicago: A. W. Bowen & Co., 1902.

Baldwin, Leland D. *The Keelboat Age on Western Waters.* Pittsburgh: University of Pittsburgh Press, 1941.

Bancroft, H. H. *History of Washington, Idaho, and Montana, 1845–89.* San Francisco: The History Company, 1890.

Bates, Alan L. *The Western Rivers Steamboat Cyclopedium.* New Jersey: Hustle Press, 1968.

Berry, Gerald E. *The Whoop-Up Trail: Early Days in Alberta-Montana.* Edmonton: Applied Art Products, 1953; reprint, Lethbridge, Alberta: Lethbridge Historical Society, 1995.

Breen, David. H. *The Canadian Prairie West and the Ranching Frontier, 1874–1924.* Toronto: University of Toronto Press, 1983.

Burlingame, Merrill G., and K. Ross Toole, eds. *A History of Montana.* New York: Lewis Historical Publishing, 1957.

Burns & Eliot Co., eds. *Calgary, Her Industry and Resources.* Calgary: Burns & Eliot Co., 1885.

Butler, W. F. *The Great Lone Land: A Narrative and Adventure in the North-West of America.* London: Low and Searle, 1873.

Cassler, Michael M. *Steamboats of the Fort Union Fur Trade.* Williston, N.D.: Fort Union Association, 1999.

Chappell, Phil E. "River Navigation: A History of the Missouri River." *Transactions of the Kansas State Historical Society, 1905–1906* 9 (1906): 226–31.

Chittenden, Hiram Martin. "Ancient Town of Fort Benton." *Magazine of Western History* (December 1890).

———. *The American Fur Trade of the Far West.* New York: Francis P. Harper, 1902.

———. *History of Early Steamboat Navigation on the Missouri River: Life and Adventures of Joseph LaBarge.* Cleveland: Arthur H. Clark, 1903.

Chouteau, Charles P. "Report of Chas. P. Chouteau to Secretary of War of a Steamboat Expedition from St. Louis to Fort Benton, 1859."*Contributions to the Historical Society of Montana* 3 (1859): 255.

Corbin, Annalies. *The Material Culture of Steamboat Passengers: Archaeological Evidence from the Missouri River.* New York: Plenum Press, 2000.

———. "Shifting Sand and Muddy Water: Historic Cartography and River Migration as Factors in Locating Steamboat Wrecks on the Far Upper Missouri River." *Historical Archaeology* 32, no. 4 (1998): 86–94.

———. "Steamboat Archaeology on the Missouri River: Searching for the Forgotten Past." In *The International Handbook of Underwater Archaeology,* edited by Carol V. Ruppe and Janet F. Barstad, IP. New York: Plenum Press, 2002, 193–206.

Corbin, Annalies, and Kenneth W. Karsmizki. "Steamboats in Montana: Wrecks of the Far Upper Missouri–Yellowstone Area." *Underwater Archaeology* (1997): 61–68.

Deatherage, Charles P. *Steamboating on the Missouri in the Sixties.* Published by the author, 1924.

Denny, Cecil E. *The Law Marches West.* Toronto: J. M. Dent and Sons, 1939.

denOtter, A. A. "The Hudson's Bay Company's Prairie Transportation Problem, 1870–1885." In *The Developing West,* edited by John E. Foster. Alberta: University of Alberta Press, 1983.

Drago, Harry Sinclair. *The Steamboaters: From Early Side-Wheelers to the Big Packets.* New York: Dodd, Mead, 1967.

Elliot, T. C. "The Mullan Road: Its Local History and Significance." *Washington Historical Quarterly* 14, no. 3 (1923): 206–209.

Fishbaugh, Charles Preston. *From Paddle Wheels to Propellers.* Indianapolis: Indiana Historical Society, 1970.

Fitch, George. "The Missouri, Its Habits and Eccentricities Described by a Personal Friend." *American Magazine* 63, no. 6 (1907).

Foster, John E., ed. *The Developing West.* Edmonton: University of Alberta Press, 1983.

Francis, James M. "Business, Enterprise, and the National Policy: the Role of T. C. Power & Brother and I. G. Baker & Company in the Political and Economic Development of the Southwestern Canadian Prairies and Northern Montana, 1870–1893." Master's thesis, University of British Columbia, 1978.

———. "Montana Business and Canadian Regionalism in the 1780s and 1880s." *Western Historical Quarterly* 12, no. 3 (1981): 291–304.

French, G. A. "Report of the Commissioner North-West Mounted Police, 1874." In *Opening Up the West: Being the Official Reports to Parliament of the Activities of the Royal Mounted Police Force from 1874–1881.* Ottawa: Maclean, Roger & Co., 1874–1881, reprinted Toronto: Cole Publishing Company, 1973.

Gamble, Jay Mack. "Up River to Benton." *Montana: The Magazine of Western History* 6, no. 2 (1956): 32–41.

Gluek, Alvin C. *Minnesota and the Manifest Destiny of the Canadian Northwest: A Study in Canadian-American Relations.* Toronto: University of Toronto Press, 1965.

Halvorson, Ora Johnson. "Charles E. Conrad of Kalispell: Merchant Prince with a Gentle Touch." *Montana: The Magazine of Western History* 21, no. 2 (1971): 56–67.

Hammer, Kenneth M. "River and Rail: Competition in the Upper-Missouri Basin." *Journal of the West* 17, no. 4 (1978): 41–51.

Hanson, Joseph Mills. *The Conquest of the Missouri: Being the Story of the Life and Exploits of Captain Grant Marsh.* New York: Murray Hill Books Inc., 1909.

Harber, Nora E. *Our Fort Benton.* Fort Benton, Mont.: River Press, [1940s].

Havighurst, Walter. "Steamboat to the Rockies." *American West* 7, no. 5 (1970): 4–11, 61–62.

Horrall, S. W. "Sir John A. Macdonald and the Mounted Police Force of the Northwest Territories." *Canadian Historical Review* 53 (1972): 179–200.

Howard, Addison. "Captain John Mullan." *Washington Historical Quarterly* 25, no. 3 (1934): 185–202.

Hunter, Louis C. *Steamboats on Western Rivers: An Economic and Technological History.* Cambridge: Harvard University Press, 1949.

Jackson, Donald. *Voyages of the Steamboat* Yellow Stone. New York: Ticknor and Fields, 1985.

Johnson, Dorothy M. "Slow Boat to Benton." *Montana: The Magazine of Western History* 11, no. 1 (1961): 2–11.

Jones, Ivan E. "Steamboating on the Nebraska Shore." *Nebraska History* 8, no. 1 (1925): 11–13.

Klassen, Henry C. "I. G. Baker and Company in Calgary, 1875–1884." *Montana: The Magazine of Western History* 35, no. 3 (1985): 40–55.

Lass, William E. *A History of Steamboating on the Upper Missouri.* Lincoln: University of Nebraska Press, 1962.

———. "Steamboating on the Missouri: Its Significance on the Northern Great Plains." *Journal of the West* 7, no. 1 (1967): 53–67.

———. *From the Missouri River to the Great Salt Lake: An Account of Overland Freighting.* Lincoln: Nebraska State Historical Society, 1972.

———. "Missouri River Steamboating." *North Dakota History* 56, no. 3 (1989): 3–15.

Leeson, Michael A., ed. *History of Montana, 1739–1885.* Chicago: Warner, Beers & Co., 1885.

Lepley, John G. "Old Reliable: The Steamboat *Benton* on the Upper Missouri." *Montana: The Magazine of Western History* 30, no. 3 (1980): 42–51.

Lytle, William M., and Forrest R. Holdcamper. *Merchant Steam Vessels of the United States 1790–1868.* New York: Steamship Historical Society, 1975.

Macleod, Roderick Charles. "The North-West Mounted Police 1873–1905: Law Enforcement and the Social Order in the Canadian North-West." Ph.D. diss., Duke University, 1971.

———. *The North-West Mounted Police 1873–1905: Law Enforcement and Social Order in the Canadian North-West.* Toronto: University of Toronto Press, 1976.

Madsen, Brigham D. "The Montana Trail: Salt Lake City–Corinne to Fort Benton." *Overland Journal* 13 (1995): 19–34.

Madsen, Brigham D., and Betty M. "The Diamond R Rolls Out." *Montana: The Magazine of Western History* 21, no. 2 (1971): 2–17.

Malone, Michael P., and Richard W. Etulain. *The American West: A Twentieth Century History.* Lincoln: University of Nebraska Press, 1989.

Malone, Michael P., Richard B. Roeder, and William L. Lang. *Montana: A History of Two Centuries.* Seattle: University of Washington Press, 1976.

McBride, Fanny Fern. "Steamboating on the Upper Missouri." Master's thesis, University of Nebraska, 1929.

McDonald, W. J. "The Missouri River and Its Victims." *Missouri Historical Review* 21 (1927): 215–42, 455–80, 581–607.

Merk, Frederick. *Manifest Destiny and Mission in American History.* New York: Alfred A. Knopf, 1963.

Miller, Joaquin. *An Illustrated History of the State of Montana.* Chicago: Lewis Publishing Co., 1894.

Montana Historical Society (MHS). "Steamboat Arrivals at Fort Benton." *Contributions to the Historical Society of Montana* 3 (1900): 352.

Murphy, James E. *Half Interest in a Silver Dollar: The Saga of Charles E. Conrad.* Missoula: Mountain Press Publishing, 1983.

Nevitt, R. B. *A Winter at Fort Macleod,* edited by Hugh A. Dempsey. Calgary, Glenbow-Alberta Institute: McClelland and Stewart West, 1974.

Norall, Frank. *Bourgmont, the Explorer of the Missouri, 1698–1725.* Lincoln: University of Nebraska Press, 1988.

Oglesby, Richard E. *Manuel Lisa and the Opening of the Missouri Fur Trade.* Norman: University of Oklahoma Press, 1963.

O'Sullivan, John. "The Nation of Futurity." *Democratic Review* 6 (1839): 426–30.

———. "Territorial Aggrandizement." *Democratic Review* 17 (1845): 243–48.

Overholser, Joel. *Fort Benton: World's Innermost Port.* Helena, Mont.: Falcon Press Publishing, 1987.

———. "The Big Muddy Builds Montana." In *Our Fort Benton,* edited by Nora E. Harber, [1940s]. Fort Benton, Mont.: River Press.

Oviatt, Alton B. "Fort Benton, River Capital." In *A History of Montana,* edited by Merrill G. Burlingame and K. Ross Toole, 137–55. New York: Lewis Historical Publishing Company, 1957.

———. "Pacific Coast Competition for the Gold Camp Trade of Montana." *Pacific Northwest Quarterly* 56, no. 4 (1965): 168–76.

Parkman, Francis. *The Oregon Trail.* Boston: Houghton Mifflin Co., 1925.

Parsons, John E. "Steamboats in the 'Idaho' Gold Rush." *Montana: The Magazine of Western History* 10, no. 1 (1960): 51–61.

Peterson, William J., ed. "The Log of the *Henry M. Shreve* to Fort Benton." *Mississippi Valley Historical Review* 31 (1945): 537–78.

Petsche, Jerome. E. *The Steamboat* Bertrand: *History, Excavation, and Architecture.* Washington, D.C.: National Park Service, 1974.

Phillips, Paul Chrisler. *The Fur Trade.* Norman: University of Oklahoma Press, 1961.

Pratt, Julius W. "John O'Sullivan and Manifest Destiny." *New York History* 14 (1933): 213–34.

Rodgers, Bradley A. *Guardian of the Great Lakes: The US Paddle Frigate.* Ann Arbor: University of Michigan Press, 1996.

Sanders, Helen Fitzgerald. *A History of Montana.* Chicago: Lewis Publishing, 1913.

Sandon, Bob, and Bunky Sullivan. "Taming the Missouri and Treating Depression: Fort Peck Dam." *Montana: The Magazine of Western History* 27, no. 3 (1977): 34–57.

Saum, Lewis O. "Stanley Huntley Interviews Sitting Bull: Event, Pseudo-Event or Fabrication?" *Montana: The Magazine of Western History* 32, no. 2 (1982): 2–15.

Schneiders, Robert Kelley. *Unruly River: Two Centuries of Change along the Missouri.* Lawrence: University of Kansas Press, 1999.

Schwantes, Carlos A. *Long Day's Journey: The Steamboat and Stagecoach Era in the Northern West.* Seattle: University of Washington Press, 1999.

Senieur, Matilda. "Bismarck to Fort Benton by Steamboat in the Year 1869." *Montana: The Magazine of Western History* 2, no. 2 (1952): 57–59.

Sharp, Paul F. "Whoop-Up Trail: International Highway on the Great Plains." *Pacific Historical Review* 21 (1952): 129–44.

———. "Merchant Princes of the Plains." *Montana: The Magazine of Western History* 5, no. 1 (1955): 2–20.

———. *Whoop-Up Country: The Canadian-American West, 1865–1885.* Norman: University of Oklahoma Press, 1978.

Sheldon, Addison E. "The Missouri River Region as Seen by the First White Explorers." *Nebraska History* 8, no. 1 (1927): 5–11.

Silliman, Lee. "Up This Great River: Daniel Weston's Missouri River Steamboat Diary." *Montana: The Magazine of Western History* 30, no. 3 (1980): 32–41.

Stout, Tom, ed. *Montana: Its Story and Biography.* Chicago: American Historical Society, 1921.

Stuart, Granville. *Forty Years on the Frontier.* Cleveland: Arthur H. Clark, 1905.

Swagerty, William R. "Indian Trade in the Trans-Mississippi West to 1870." In *History of Indian-White Relations, Vol. 4, Handbook of North American Indians,* edited by Wilcomb E. Washburn and William C. Sturtevant. Washington, D.C.: Smithsonian Institution, 1988.

Utley, Robert M. "The Dash to Promontory." *Utah Historical Quarterly* 29, no. 2 (1961): 98–117.

Vestal, Stanley. *The Missouri.* Lincoln: University of Nebraska Press, 1945.

Way, Frederick, Jr. *Way's Packet Directory, 1848–1994.* Athens: University of Ohio Press, 1983.

Weinberg, Albert K. *Manifest Destiny.* Baltimore: The Johns Hopkins Press, 1935.

West, Carroll Van. "Coulson and the Clark's Fork Bottom." *Montana: The Magazine of Western History* 35, no. 4 (1985): 42–55.

Winther, Oscar Osburn. "Early Commercial Importance of the Mullan Road." *Oregon Historical Quarterly* 46, no. 1 (1945): 22–35.

———. *The Transportation Frontier, Trans-Mississippi West, 1865–1890.* New York: Holt, Rinehart, and Winston, 1964.

Wood, Asa A. "Fort Benton's Part in the Development of the West." *Washington Historical Quarterly* 10, no. 3 (1929): 213–22.

Index

Italicized page numbers refer to images.